DEEP IN THE HEART
OF TEXAS

DEEP IN THE HEART OF TEXAS

A MEMOIR

TEXAS A. STREADY

Published by A Radical Difference

Cover design by Samira Gast Myers.

Samira Gast Myers is an artist and public speaker. She is also the founder of the Dear Cannon Art Project, a non profit that provides art education programs where funding has been cut. Find out more at www.samiragastmyers.com.

Cathee A. Poulsen, Editor

Printed in USA
American Print Resources, LLC
www.americanprintresources.com
Seventh Printing: March 2020
11,800 copies in circulation

ISBN: 978-0-578-21374-3

Library of Congress Catalog Card Number: 2018914546

To my parents, who gave so much of their lives that I may be free.

To my glorious children, who have not only endured but become champions of life.

To my sister-in-law Dorothy, who has loved me and believed in me no matter what.

To my sister Dori, whose example taught me to keep fighting.

TABLE OF CONTENTS

ACKNOWLEDGEMENTS

Mom, you are my biggest fan, besides my grandsons, of course. You have tirelessly put up with me and without doubt taught me everything I know about writing. Couldn't have done it without you.

Polly, thank you for your hours of faithful reading with diligent and open-minded discernment. You're the bomb.

Lissa, thanks for the endless supply of paper in the CCJ, when I first started this book.

A NOTE TO THE READER

This is a memoir. It reflects my recollection of life experiences. Certain names, locations and identifying qualities are composites, meant to get my point across without causing shame or controversy. Dialogue and events have been compressed to convey the substance of what was said and done.

TO THE AFRICAN-AMERICAN

I want to make crystal clear that the parts of my book address-ing my relationship with the black community are in no way meant to degrade, be a reflection of, or stereotype this race as a whole. An element of evil exists in all people. I know an equal amount of absolutely incredible black men and women, that not only love the Lord with a depth we know nothing of, they have a respect and bond with each other that white folks can't touch. So many deeply wounded areas of my life have been healed due to my connection with this culture. Thank you to all the friends and family I have gained on my journey through the projects. Wouldn't trade it for nothin'.

TO THE CHRISTIAN

There's no neat escape from sin. Entrapment's highway is easier to follow than freedom's path. The Bible promises grace for the needy and if this lifestyle is foreign to you, you'll need grace to comprehend the reality of my story.

Truth is, we all have sin that alters our relationship with Christ. Even if it's socially accepted, it cannot be tolerated by a perfect God. Without Jesus there's no freedom. He came to seek and save *all* the lost. He searches us out right in the middle of our sin. The nasty, filthy, disrespectful hole of bad choices.

Today my prayer is: God, may I never think I'm so clean I forget what dirty feels like.

If we don't know how sin tricks people, what their battles look like, or why they run to their sin of choice, how will we do what Christ commanded? *Go where they live and tell them who I Am.*

There are people whose lives depend on hearing the truth God's given me. Most are incapable of receiving it in a pretty little package. Open your mind. Not in agreement with this lifestyle but in agreement with meeting people where they live. God's grace is huge. He has no illusions about us. He's fully aware of *all* our sin.

If this book is too much for you, that's okay. But you having it is no accident—too much prayer for that. Someone you know is desperate for truth. Share it!

PROLOGUE

$\int$ ilent as I wait on her arrival. A warm excitement rises from my chest to my shoulders. Adrenaline stomps up the back of my neck. It pushes a hefty load of heart-throbbing anticipation that rinses my mind of all other thought. My life spins its existence in search of the high that only she can take me to.

The five minutes of preparation and two minutes of application took forever. That part's over. She's on her way up the drive. All aboard! Here comes the cocaine train.

Rushing sounds gain volume the closer the mix of blood gets to my brain. Screaming sirens reverberate through my skull like a struck gong. The locomotive slams through the wall and into the bathroom where I've tied my gray arm to the tracks in an unintended suicide attempt.

Her power captivates me with a dazzling crown of mixed emotion. The freedom she offers is temporary—a dangerous gamble.

Pain that once called for stitches, now demands surgery. Her promise to heal has no relevance. All she offers is a Band-Aid. But for now, that will do.

Fear's powerful presence is a must when shooting cocaine. If it's not right at too much, it's nowhere near enough.

Warm and familiar flavor fills my throat. Umm, oh so good.

Fear tips his hat. The air grows thick. Sight fades in and out as if some kid's discovered a dimmer switch. Waves of bubbling ecstasy wash over my face and chest. My legs vibrate. I sit on the toilet to keep from collapse. Wow! Awesome! I love it.

My brain beats. My senses shake. Take it easy. Slow down. Relax.

I knew by the color of the liquid I drew, it was a risky amount. But this life begs for risk. Was that too much? How stupid. It's not stopping. Too much. Oh my god—too much.

Paralyzed by millions of thoughts. When will the climb level off? Is this gonna kill me? Why in the world do I do it? Will God save me or have I gone too far?

I'm in trouble but can't call homeboy from the kitchen. He already shared his stuff and has no clue I have more. Skimmed hard off his package before he ever saw it. Hey, I don't sell drugs to make friends.

Who cares if he's mad? I need help. Better him mad than me dead. Yell, Texas.

Can't even push a moan up and out. No body parts work right at the moment. Shower. I need the shower.

I drop my head between my knees to gain some sort of composure. Voices in my skull are loud but unclear. My soul reaches out to grab my body. It scratches to hold on but there are no muscles to support it.

Pounding, pounding, pounding.

My heart's gonna explode. *God, please don't let me die. Please!*

I attempt to drag myself into the tub but end up face down on the tile beside the toilet. There's a puddle of blood. I tore my thumbnail off on the way down. Didn't even feel it.

The florescent light that was too bright seconds ago is now dim. Like a cloud drifted over it. Through the haze I see my fingers clinched around my rig. I'm gonna die in this damn bathroom with a syringe in my fist.

I'm in a downward spiral. You can't have me. I'm not yours. Stop. Let me go. Please stop.

My fight for escape is weak in comparison to the strength I hear in their speech. They laugh and hiss. Scream in delight one moment and mumble of doom the next. Words are unclear but my intended destination is sure. Demons drag me. I have no power. I'm in serious trouble. The room goes black and then, as if printed on the Sunday school chalkboard, I see a Bible verse.

"Those who call upon the name of the Lord shall be saved."

The room expands and encloses around me with each breath. My pulse taps on the back of my tongue like a clock that keeps time by the millisecond. Captured by the sound of mischievous chatter, horror grabs my throat, but still I say it.

"Jesus, Jesus, Jesus." Can't think or speak one other word. Just "Jesus."

Minutes inch past. Finally, I can sit up. My back rests against the wall and I attempt to settle myself down. That was close. Better knock this shit off.

Stable enough to wipe up the bloody mess and throw the equipment under the sink. I head for the front room. I need a Newport.

My hands quake as I pull a smoke from the kelly green box. Mike's at the stovetop in search of crack crumbs; guess he cooked the rest of the powder up to make crack. Fine by me. At least he's not staring. Can't handle that—too high.

The anxiety that accompanies the comedown rushes me to the porch to light up.

What's wrong with me? Will I ever find my way out of this? Can't help but wonder, how did I get here in the first place?

1

THERE WAS A LITTLE GIRL

There was a little girl
Who had a little curl,
Right in the middle of her forehead;
When she was good,
She was very, very good;
But when she was bad—she was horrid.

*W*onder if you know anyone like me. I'm sure you do. My story's not so different. It goes up-n-down, back-n-forth, and side-to-side. All the while I'm left hanging in the balance. Without any balance.

Texas. That's my name. Texas, like the state. Yes, it's my real name. No, I was not born there. I was born in Miami, Florida. Wasn't conceived there either. The reason my name is Texas is because my grandfather was born there. My mother grew up hearing, "Texas this and Texas that. Everything's bigger and better in Texas." One day she said, "If I ever have a daughter I will name her Texas," and she did.

I've quoted these ten lines to people more than you can imagine. Children on playgrounds, teachers in classrooms. Employers, coworkers. Men in bars, friends at church. Officers, inmates, sinners and saints. Anyone who hears my name.

Miami in the 60s was not what it is today, or so I'm told. I was born there but left right after my first birthday. No memories. In my head Miami howls par-tay—not till I return at seventeen—but that's what I recall of the spot.

My parents Robert and Cathleen Poulsen were born in Miami. Raised there too. They graduate, are married, and there they give birth to Buddy and me. Curtis and Jed come later.

Mom and Dad attend Florida Bible College in nearby Coconut Grove. They're what people refer to as, "sold out to Jesus."

★ ★ ★

My teenage years are spent with my fingers crammed so far down my ears they begin to gag me. North Carolina's different. It's my father's first church. Not sure what's what. Not just yet.

Mom's worried and rushed. Busy with the new baby. Raised to believe that value is found in performance, she drives us with this same concept. Cathee works hard to get there. Wherever *there* is. She loves me, but it's out of duty not desire. She doesn't snuggle up to me like my dad does. This opens the cavity between us where decay begins.

"Daddy's home, Daddy's home."

The cheers begin the moment he cracks the front door. The middle of the living room floor is where he lays, and like ants who have discovered a neglected bite of gingerbread, my brother and I climb all over him. We work hard to avoid his agile grip. A dash, a dart, a lunge, a leap. It's by far my favorite time of day.

The smell of cornbread drifts from the kitchen as the three of us scramble about shouting and screaming.

Mother yells, "Bob—stop that! Someone's going to get hurt."

She's on a personal mission to make me unhappy. Careful, proper, uptight Mom. Forever following the rules and missing the fun. Boring.

Dad doesn't stop the horseplay. Not until she comes barreling out. Checked apron swung low, wooden spoon held high, she demands sternly, "Bob! Stop!"

The parsonage sits close to the brick church. From our front porch you can spit and hit the steps. If your aim is on. Our wooden house is matchbox flimsy. It looks as if the congregation themselves erected it. Three modest bedrooms and a tiny bathroom.

Dad does repairs outside and inside Mom keeps everything in perfect place. Fresh flowers on the table where hot raisin bread cools in the glow of a mulberry-scented, homemade candle.

On Sundays, Momma and the three of us sit two rows back to the right of the pulpit while Daddy gives his sermon. This particular week something deep within absorbs the usual distractions. No doodles. No whispers. Ears switched on high. When people are invited to come and accept Jesus, I ache with envy. But jitters keep me tacked to the wooden pew like B'rer Rabbit to the Tar Baby.

After lunch I notice Daddy at rest in his favorite chair. I slide under his relaxed arm and nuzzle in close to his toasty side.

"I want Jesus to live in my heart, Daddy." I announce. He shifts about and moves me to the center of his lap. Our eyes become fastened. No convincing or explaining needed. I'm fully persuaded. My heart's been altered. Dad takes a moment to reinforce the important specifics of this decision, then leads me in prayer.

At five years old—in the center of our homey living space, resting safe in the arms of my hero—I ask Jesus to be my savior.

We live at the corner of a state road and a poorly-paved side street. Both directions offer hours of timeless fun. Down the slope of the front yard across the safe street stands a two-story white house. The green trim was once fresh and shiny. Now it looks more like a weathered garden hose.

Mrs. Laws is the owner of this cozy environment. To my knowledge she has no children or living relatives. Her husband died years before we came. Although her voice and attitude never reflect sadness, somewhere in her squirrel-colored eyes I can tell she needs us. Life for her has softly settled into a small area of the house.

Inside the kitchen door to the right are the usual applianc-es. Refrigerator, stove and sink. A round table cramped with four chairs neighbor them.

"Darling, will you hand me the bed controller?" she says. An electric twin bed has overtaken the former dining area. Never been to a hospital, so this bed amazes me. Since then I've held tight to many an electric bed, mainly for reason of detox. Funny thing, they all offer the same safety and support found here.

What's left of the space is congested with two thin book-shelves, and what looks like a child's wooden desk. The bath-room's down the hall. These three rooms prove all our fragile friend needs.

The rest of the house goes untouched. Fascinating. For a kid anyway. What was once a grand establishment is now a mysterious trunk full of dust-covered secrets from yesteryear.

Mrs. Laws never attends church. She's kind and gentle though. "The church house is not for me, children," she insists, "but I'm glad you kids enjoy it."

"Can we play in the yard, Mrs. Laws?"

"As long as your parents don't mind, baby. Remember, I'm not the boss."

Her huge yard is captivating. Ancient oaks, poplars, and maples. Autumn ushers in various majestic shades. Russet reds, royal purples and golden ambers, English ivy spiraled tight to each trunk. Trees appear to unite arms in allegiance against the sun creating a magical air of excitement. Discovery's light dances through narrow gaps in the canopy. It shines hope on the cool dim earth below.

Further down the yard, a shallow brook covers a delightful world of surprises. Oval stones as slick as an otter's belly. Minnows and tadpoles rush about in search of food or shelter. Anxious crawdads hide under rocks, while sleek salamanders dart to and fro like a pinball racking up points. On occasion we run across an overweight toad cooling his toes in the flow of the stream. The majority of our playtime is spent here, engulfed in utter fascination.

On days of good fortune, Mom watches from the porch while we venture in the other direction. My little brother, Curtie, is rarely allowed to cross the big street, so Buddy and I—six and eight—are on our own. Once beyond the highway, we wave to Mom. Then up the snake-shaped drive we bolt.

"Bye-bye! See you later," we shout.

The gravel ends on the edge of wealth and splendor. A three-story, crisp white Victorian palace, trimmed in lobster red with shutters to match.

"Can I get you kids some dates or cider," Mrs. Carpenter asks.

"Not today, thank you. We're in a hurry." Down the path we scamper.

A tad beyond the house—before the worn tractor trail—stands an old cobblestone springhouse. The water comes up from the ground and flows through a homemade filtration system. It drips at a steady pace into a basin. Once full, the overflow returns to its original entrance. To retrieve a drink, you dip a hollowed gourd into the pool of crystal-clear water.

"Hey Buddy, know how you get the best water? You wait for the drip to fill the gourd, that's how." I long to be special, or at least impress.

Breath held tight, hearts skip in anticipation. We unlatch the gate to the great barn. I say great, not because of how it looks, or where it stands. No, no, it's greatness is found inside. Diced into individual stalls, it houses three immensely over-rated donkeys. Jake is the tallest and most ornery—the leader of the pack. Lil Jon is a tame, easygoing guy. And Joey? He won't be saddled or ridden.

The aroma of manure, laced with oats, joins the sweet smell of hay. It surrounds me the closer I get. One whiff transports my heart to a place as intriguing as Alice's Wonderland. The sharp smell of leather rules the air, and to this day—be it boot shop or purse gallery—one whiff brings me here.

The tattered barn door is propped open with an old horse shoe. Exhilaration causes my legs to feel like tulip stems, all hollow and watery. A lopsided tractor lives in a pile of mud before the barn. Whoever tags it first rides Lil' Jon. Buddy's rule.

The competition is never announced so distracting him is my only shot. On rare and brilliant occasions, I divert his attention and with a head start I seize my victory.

"I win. I win. Lil' Jon is mine today."

We learn to do the work required to ride these pets. Up steep hills, through wild brush, across rocky streams. With a running start you can leap over fallen branches if they aren't too high; otherwise you drag them. The two of us remove many a downed branch due to a headstrong burro. We ride these barn-sour animals with great glee as often as permitted.

I look back with fondness on these years of imagination and adventure.

Childhood passes and virtue runs behind it. The world in this pokey country town is secure. Not like the next place. The one that abducts my purity.

Innocent.

2

WHO'S NIBBLING

Nibble, nibble, mousekin,
Who's nibbling at my housekin?

"Paper or plastic?" The Winn-Dixie cashier doesn't ask this. There's no such thing as plastic grocery bags. Not yet. Toting groceries isn't as easy, but Halloween requires paper bags. Soldier, angel, villain or vixen. From swords to stars—-details make good costumes, and where we live, they're cut from paper bags. Adults draw better patterns and cut straighter lines but in this neighborhood parents are kinda like plastic bags. Not around.

Leaving North Carolina was sad. We're back in Florida. Melbourne. We live in a subdivision called Sherwood Park. No, it's not a trailer park, but the middle to lower class residents are what some would classify as "trailer trash."

Wrong makes no distinction between race, religion or riches. People use labels sarcastically in hopes of camouflaging their own dirt. It's mean, but it seems everyone does it.

Locksley Road glows with street lamps, flashlights and jack-o-lanterns. The atmosphere is warm, dark and exciting, like sneaking a sip from Daddy's coffee mug.

Marvin Carter's creative blood runs thicker than most. An older boy from a few streets down, Marv has an unusual idea for paper bags. Dressed in black, his naughty smile is as bright as tonight's full moon. Buddy and Curtis take off in the opposite direction for trick-or-treat. I stay to watch Marvin. Too innocent for fear.

"What are you dressed as, Marv?" I ask. "And why do you smell?"

"None of your beeswax. Run along little church girl."

Pretending to scout-out my brothers, I duck behind the Marinetti's shrubs. The usual symphony of crickets is silent, as if they're in on it. A fuel-soaked bag drops in the Kelly's carport. Scotty Trapan strikes the lighter while Marvin rings the doorbell. Then like fish when a rock hits the water, they're gone. Vanished

The Mr. bolts from the house in a panic-filled rage, his overly-tall wife close behind. Stomp, splat, splash, goes Edward Kelly's red slipper. I wait in the brush, praying his pants don't catch fire. The sloppy brown mound's a stinky mess.

Mrs. Kelly grabs the hose. The flames die out but the odor lives on.

"Dammit, Myrtle. The bag is full of horse crap. Can't ya smell it? Now-a-days kids have no upbringin'."

Can't stop the laughter. What a thrill. I take off to catch my brothers. Don't want to miss the Shepherd's place. They give Reeses and Snickers.

The best part of living here? Kids are everywhere. A strange land. Children talk back to adults while women smoke cancer sticks and men dip Skoal and spit. Right in front of the church. Back in North Carolina, Mr. Hayward chewed long smelly strings of tobacco. When finished, he'd scoop the load from his cheek and sling it into an old Folger's can. But never at church.

Real life romps up and down our street. Divorced parents yell and throw things. Delinquent kids say cuss words and steal stuff. There's even alcoholic criminals on probation.

If gifted enough to be a minister of the gospel, you're subject to the move of the Holy Spirit. That's how we got here. Personally, I think the program can use a revamp. The job description is enormous, the incentive plan leaves much to be desired, and the pay scale bites. Besides, you're always left considering what God's up to? Who wants to work for that sort of organization? Not me.

The Bible story of poor Job tells you things aren't exactly as they appear. Job had it all and for no good reason he's stripped butt-naked and left with nothing but pus-filled sores. Who the heck cares if he ends up on the plus side. The blatant disregard for his feelings is cold. No doubt the Board of Directors had something to do with it.

The amazing thing? I don't get mad at God. Jesus chose to die to spare my life. He obviously cares. Not only that, He's killed by His own people. The ones He's trying to help. At ten, I figure God just bit off a little more than He could chew, dealing with these churchgoers.

Sunday evenings we rush home for Little House on the Prairie. Dad comes in later. He heads straight to the study. Something's wrong. The show ends and the boys mosey off to ready themselves for bed. Down the hallway I follow the worn blue carpet to his office. Peeking around the door I see Daddy, head resting heavy in his hands, Bible open on the Army-green metal desk. Distressed.

"You okay?" I softly say.

My slim body slips with ease between the desk and chair. I wiggle my way into his lap. Poking at the perfect spots, he gives me a tickle or two. Both arms around his neck in reassurance, I say in a doubtless tone, "Jesus will take care of it, Daddy."

Then off to bed I scamper. I fall asleep to a jumble of Mother's worried questions, pulsed to the beat of the Hawaii-Five-O drum.

People in Florida are way smarter than we are. There are conditions, challenges and circumstances. Ideas, issues and incidents. Things I've never heard of. My parents are kind, honest, hard-working people. That isn't what makes them different. It's the God thing. Everyone's not like them. Some even think they're ridiculous. I don't want to be ridiculous.

Growing up we memorize scriptures, sing songs and hear Bible stories. Before dinner we hold hands and bless the food. Upon release, arms fly in search of the biggest biscuit or fattest chicken leg. Evening is spent on homework first. Then television or games.

Bob and Cathee thrust their entire lives into ministry. They leave college on assignment to introduce the world to Jesus Christ. They're sure the planet is lost and dying, when in fact it's ready and waiting with a whole different plan in mind.

Rick and Rita are always around. They live at the end of the street. Their mom works two jobs since her husband left. He's not their dad but pretty close. They call him, Mr. Dangry cause he drinks and gets angry. Now that he's absent, they can't decide which is worse. Drunk or gone.

My younger brother and I have an alliance. "We need to hang tight. Two is better than one when it comes to Buddy," I say. Still, I'm on my own a lot. Curtis is smart enough to steer clear but keeping up with Buddy is everything to me.

Our one car garage doesn't house the family station wagon. Instead it holds supplies. Stuff to patch, restore or remodel anything. Projects Mom insists on. New wallpaper for the kitchen, a dog house for the back yard, or a table alongside the dryer.

"Clothes will have less wrinkles if I fold them here," she informs. Dad builds everything without flaw.

Wood of every size and shape, hand tools, power tools, a million nails and screws—all sorted and filed in proper place. Paints, glues and oils rest on one shelf, while vases, pots and fertilizer reclines on another.

Ricky and Buddy coax us into a variety of new and stimulating activities. Things we know we shouldn't do. That's how we learned this trick. In the front right corner of this orderly space, behind the rolling door, the lawnmower waits. A red aluminum tin stamped GASOLINE is close by. Rita and I sneak in and shimmy up to it.

Pinched between a stack of concrete blocks and some drywall, I remove the rusty lid and place my mouth and nose as close as the container allows. Hands cupped around my face and over the opening, I breathe—in and out, in and out—as long and hard as my lungs will pull. Faster and faster I huff the fumes until the burn of breakfast rises in my throat.

Stillness awakens. Waves of warped sound and sight. Fuzzy objects twitch as if they live, providing a thirty second lapse in time. Back and forth we pass the gas can in attempts to continue enchantment's dance.

"It's my turn," I complain. Rita wants to stop long before I do.

The mental merry-go-round twists and turns bringing fresh zest to an otherwise dull afternoon.

★ ★ ★

"Your mom is pregnant."

"What? A baby?" I shriek.

I'm sickened by the possibility of a sister. Being the only girl is all I have. Fright rules my imagination for nine long months until six pound, six ounce, Jedediah Dunlap slides into home.

I wake one morning to Dad's excited shake. "Guess what? You have a baby brother."

"A brother? Thank God!" I shout.

Crazy about Jed. He gives me importance. It's like a live babydoll. He needs me and my love for him is huge. Intense. Even more fun than Church Fellowships.

Monthly dinner on the grounds, holiday parties, ice-cream-churning socials, and pie eating competitions. We get as full as a homeless man's stolen shopping cart. Church people can be judgmental but church activities are what we live for.

Picnics at Wickham Park are the best. Parents get involved. Grilled burgers, baked beans, and potato salad. Never once does Miss Parrish forget to bring marshmallow fries, dipped in chocolate. My favorite.

The Stole's have a volleyball net. "Hey kids, go set this up in the lake."

"In the middle of the lake? Cool. Let's go," Buddy yells.

Such fun. But for me, the best thing here are the horses. Since my first cowboy flick I've wanted one. Although Texas brings a cowgirl to mind, in my heart I'm an Indian. I feel for them. Danger, hardship, grief. I hate the injustice of it all.

The bold orange sun fades into the tall Australian pines. Around a roaring bonfire we sing hymns full voice, with great conviction, bringing a perfect day to a peaceful end.

My eleventh birthday brings fantasy to life. Mom and Dad buy me my very own horse. Can't believe it. I do matter. You'd think I'd have each detail in place but as I attempt to replay the event, it's lost. Swallowed by a deceitful and overpowering perception of insignificance.

Boundaries are getting blurred, leaving me with incorrect conclusions. God has an agenda. He loves me and all, but like my parents, His extravagant pre-formulated plan is all that counts. What matters to me is small compared to the big stuff. My folks are too committed to neglect their God-given responsibility. That's okay. I'll just take care of me.

Ignorance.

3

UP THE HILL

The grand old Duke of York,
He had ten thousand men;
He marched them up the hill one day,
And marched them down again.
And when they were up, they were up,
And when they were down, they were down,
And when they were only half-way up,
They were neither up nor down.

Foggy about the incident that brings sex to life, all I'm sure is it wasn't my idea. I don't mind though. In fact, I'm thrilled to discover there are things boys can't do alone. In this matter, I matter. I'm a girl. Young but smart, and I have manipulating skills a car salesman would patent. It doesn't take long to figure out that I have the goods and therefore the power.

How will people treat me if they know I like it? Not the sex part but the control. I'll be taken out with the trash and forgotten forever.

Through his bedroom window one afternoon, Dad overhears my brothers and I talking about masturbation and tongue kissing. He hollers, "What are you guys doing out there? Get in this house." We're in trouble now.

A waterfall of humiliation pours over me as I enter the house. We sit on the couch awaiting certain execution. It never comes. The oxygen rejoins the room when Dad enters asking. "How was school today, you guys?"

No scolding grants permission for these games to continue.

I have my first orgasm at ten, brought on by dry-humping Rita in the closet. By eleven I'm kissing boys in places no child's lips should be. Evil's gaining ground. There's a fulfillment in it that makes ignorance easy to enjoy.

Experiences affect relationship development. Self-worth's a casualty of childhood sexual encounters—consensual or abusive. When immature morals are compromised, shame rushes in to build a shady cabin of hushed lies.

At dinner one night, Dad announces that First Baptist Church Key West wants us. I'm excited for the clean slate. Getting crazy around here.

The sun rises or sets over the ocean depending which coast of Florida you choose. The Keys offer the best of both shores. Neon pink, florescent purple and ripe peach beam through the sky with beauty that stills you.

The parsonage here is huge. Nicer than anywhere we've ever lived. There's even a screened-in pool. Killer!

Like open-mouthed babes, the people in Key West will try anything. And afterwords, there's no telling what foul content might come flying up and out. A different planet, where cash matters. Gotta have it to be this laid back. The let-it-all-hang-out capital of the state.

A year and a half and we're outta there. My parents are more in touch. They don't want us influenced by this mindset. They have no knowledge of the sex stuff. Still happening—new boys.

The attacks on Dad seem more harsh and controlling. I see now that my perception was off. I'm a typical little girl in love with her perfect daddy.

Mom's who I'm mad at. She takes me places and buys me things. She wants me happy but it's almost like I bug her. I don't get it. I'm her kid. Why doesn't she like me? On top of that, she always has what she swears is the answer. This makes it easy to blame her when things don't go as planned.

My father endures life under the microscope for 12 years. By the time we land in Naples he's out of breath. Imperfection snuck up and punched him in the gut. The entire religious program stinks of cow dung to me. It's no longer good news or saving grace. More like masters in search of excuses to abuse their slaves, or good people who've plainly misunderstood the barter. A different direction may do us some good.

My father becomes supervisor of construction for a large company.

"Dad, are you done being a preacher?"

"Well Texas, that's not where God has me right now."

I'm okay with it. Maybe forfeit will bring freedom.

Naples, Florida is an affluent town. Our house is brand spankin' new. Talk about a fresh start. Money matters here too, but in a different way. The people are snotty. Everyone's trying to outdo the next. No clue what this will mean for us.

We attend Calvary Baptist Church. The building is in the heart of the city. Big and beautiful. They have no pastor so Dad is asked to fill-in as interim. Guess we're not free. Worst of all, these people are bitterly intrusive and judgmental. Not sure when I went from being a nice girl aimed at pleasing her parents, to what the Baptists call a "wayward child." Maybe I was born that way.

By thirteen the problems sound like this.

"Texas, your jeans are too tight."

"Why do you sit on the back row?"

"That's much too much make-up."

"Stop flirting with those boys."

Don't doubt there's truth in their complaints but everything gets noticed at church. What I look like, how I speak, who my friends are, my grades. I bet the deacon's committee documented my first period, for heaven's sake.

Being even a part-time pastor's daughter provides an audience. It's my job to entertain with the unexpected. Isn't it? Whatever I do, the church calls sinful, shameful or satanic. Rebellion grows arms when I determine to show them how far bad can reach.

★ ★ ★

Nowhere in Florida is more prestigious than Naples. Perfectly manicured yards, malls, and medians. The presentation is flawless. Dignified. All the class one aspires to achieve. Extravagant to the utmost.

On scholarship at a private Christian school. I don't fit in. At all. We don't come from money and you can tell. That's what classmates say. Ignored by parents, used by boys, and criticized by self. I'm used to feeling crummy but this type of hurt is different. Hateful.

Right off the bat I determine this school's not for me. I fill the bubbles on the entrance exam making an attractive pattern—hoping for excommunication. This gets me held back a year. In class pictures I was already the one in the back row, stationed alongside the teacher. Now I could be mistaken for an Amazon.

Hard work and straight A's moves me back to my proper class. Yahoo. Our scholarship requires we clean bathrooms and hallways after school on Fridays. Humiliating. One more thing to love about Christians.

Six foot four inches tall in the ninth grade, the basketball coach takes interest in Buddy. Natural ability, drive to fit in, and excellent training cause him to shine. Before I know it, the whole school knows and loves ole' Buddy-boy. My brother donates no attention my way, so the occasional profit of stealing his thunder will have to do.

Maybe I can be a cheerleader. Not as pretty or skinny as the other girls, but I'm tall. During tryouts I hear the team captain say. "Vote yes for her. We need a base." What's a base? I wonder. Until I find myself on the bottom of every pyramid. Not exactly a jazzy role.

I'm not well-developed. No period yet. The only place I have added padding is on my backside.

"Bertha-butt. Big-booty-Judy."

At recess, jarring names whip through the air like a Coke bottle in a hurricane. Careless and brutal. Even Buddy calls me, Tex-Ass, in front of his older, cooler friends. These words sting. Like a minibike muffler that lands on your inner calf, the burn of embarrassment goes deep.

The problem compounds in seventh grade when my face sprouts acne. You'd think someone planted it and had been fertilizing it for years. I'm a natural born picker, so tiny skin imperfections end up sores. A scary site, I do confess.

Junior year, my brother's a basketball legend. He begs my parents toward public school in hopes of a college scholarship. True to form I wail and moan until I'm allowed to go as well. From as far back as my brain can see, I encourage, help, or defend my brother. Trouble is, older brothers don't like that. So right in the center of my adoration for Buddy, spite begins to breathe, "Buddy's the reason for your troubles."

The more notice King Buddy receives, the louder the voice becomes.

High school can be murderous on one's self-view. I'm not all that rad, as the surfers say, but at least I'm Buddy Poulsen's sister. He crashes on the public school scene leading them to a basketball championship. I make do dancing around in his shadow. But on the inside I'm lost. Lonely. With no clue and no cure.

Facts become fragmented. The hurt of exclusion kills hope and breeds defiance. My young reasoning uses these grounds to determine what's most important. Finding a way to feel better. That's what.

Life lacks value. Nothing's on purpose. Highs and lows are everywhere. Like most kids, I've gotten pretty good at avoiding the bottom of the barrel. But not without constant concern. Not until I happen along the enjoyment of no lows.

High.

4

A GREAT FALL

Humpty Dumpty sat on a wall,
Humpty Dumpty had a great fall.
All the king's horses and all the king's men
Couldn't put Humpty together again.

Barron Collier High School educates the Who's Who of Collier County. Don't know how we landed in it's district. The wealthy are good at forming boundaries. All's well, if you stay on your own side of the fence. Not fitting in hurts. In life there's no such thing as a level playing field. This biased concept bugs me.

Elizabeth and William Peak are rich yuppies. They pretty much run the school. Once Liz wore twelve days worth of different shoes. I counted. I'm lucky to get through a week without repeating an article of clothing. I do my best to create the latest looks with hand-me-downs, dye, or a sewing kit. The American way. Dress it up and pretend it's perfect. If only this worked. The crud of life seeps through the cracks, marring our best-dressed personas.

Times are tough, church is work, school's a blah. Teachers are pleasant, classmates friendly, even my grades are good. If I get a detention or called out in youth group, it's for being late, or talking in class. Stuff like that. No enemies, but no close friends either.

Prejudice builds a wall between the haves and the have nots. On top of this wall is where the surfers hang. Bleachy hair, flip flops, worn jeans, and tie-died tee-shirts. What they have, where they live, or how they get there means nothing to them. Or anyone else for that matter.

They hang out at Mama Mia's. A pizzeria. It's the only place I love to be anymore. All my life there's been people who accidentally call me Houston or Dallas. The way I remind people is by saying, "Texas, the whole state." This particular crowd calls me, "Texas—the whole state." Probably because they stay high. Potheads. Doesn't bother me. At least they're funny. To me it seems they're the ones who enjoy life.

People with difficulties tend to flock to me. The girl who cares. When in a jam and need a plan, I have the answer. Helping people excites me. Promotes position. To the potheads I'm important. Not left out or looked down on. They have too many secrets of their own to guard. I become the help-you-up, clean-you-up, drive-you-home girl. I'll even sneak you in and lie to your parents if need be. But no drugs or alcohol for me.

Samantha's a new girl at church. She just moved from Alabama to her mom's. A country girl. Her father's had enough. Drugs, sex, and rock-n-roll. That's what she's about. Until eleventh grade, drugs didn't cross my mind. Ever. Got drunk once at the beginning of sixteen, but the spin and puke deal left a bad taste in my mouth. That ended that.

Samantha and I become friends. One Wednesday night, after church, we go to the movies. We get there early and drive to the end of the street. I leave Sammy in the car and walk to the ocean so she can roll a joint without my questions.

Off come my sandals. Sand crunches between my toes. Can't stand dirty feet, but sand is different. Love the beach. Until a few feet from the seashore, the water is as blue as the horse on a Polo shirt. Whitecaps rhythmically crash on the beach, leaving a foam that brings whipped cream to mind—the kind you spray.

Wonder if she's done yet. Don't want to be late for the movie. My feet are heavy beneath the thick sand as I shuffle back towards the parking lot. Vision is limited. The overcast leaves no moon in sight. I wiggle my toes feeling for the asphalt. Sam's lighter blazes up in the far corner of the otherwise empty parking lot. That's where I head.

I wonder what it's like to smoke pot?

By the time I reach her, a helpless grin is parked on her face. If it makes you that happy, it can't be all bad.

Still unsure, I squeeze out the words. "Let me hit that."

A quick head-turn reveals her hazel eyes staring with the intensity of Linda Blair from The Exorcist.

"No way! You serious?"

"Would I joke about that? Hand it over," I bark back in a convincing tone.

With an oh-well shrug, she points her pinched fingers my way.

"Don't hit it too hard. It's good. Don't want you dying on me out here," she snickers.

Strong smoke fills my lungs. Reminds me of standing too close to a campfire. Smoldering wood scratches your throat the same way. I blow the smoke out fast and cough. Hard. My lungs ache. Fighting for breath I push the joint in Sam's direction. No regard for the copper glow on the tip. She fumbles about trying not to get burnt.

"Hey, watch out!" She yells. My need for air takes precedence over her safety. Sam grabs it from me and we burst into laughter. So much fun. Love at first toke. Weed's nothing like alcohol; a harsh cough is tolerable in light of the fun to follow.

The peaceful hum of mind brought on by pot dispels my usual suspense-filled doubt. My arms are heavy like a boy in his first set of football pads. Unsteady, yet filled with delight. The two mile drive and walk to the ticket booth never happen in my head. I do, however, remember the trip to the snack bar. Giggling, giggling. About dumb stuff. The way my feet look when I walk, the girl's hair in the Pepsi ad, how loose change feels in my palm. Humor's found everywhere. And the snacks? Who can choose?

The theater seems darker than normal. I feel my way to the back row. Need two vacant seats. I see some, but they're right in the center. I stumble down the narrow path. Too self-absorbed to apologize for my tight rope act. Without regard for those around I collapse into a chair. I reserve Sammy's seat by pulling it down and stuffing my purse inside.

Sam turns the corner into the dark room and scans the aisles in search of me. "Over here, dumb-ass. I'm over here." There's no restraint in my voice. Volume or verbiage.

Spent most of my life performing but rarely does it end in applause. The belief that I'll get it right someday is becoming a joke in my self-mutilating mind. In my burdensome attempts for approval, the flare of who cares lights a fresh path that encourages my exhausted heart. Like the relief of a damp rag after a long run, anxiety's cooled.

Sore from laughter and undaunted by the world around me, I'm keen with the comebacks. If not, it doesn't matter. Nothing matters much. Intrigued by this unique encounter with ease. I'm grateful. Never knew life could be so breezy. Instantly entranced. Can't see that I'm soaring top speed towards a hopeless life of stormy dreams with rainy endings.

Ironic. Three hours of fake freedom leave me caught in three decades of real bondage. All I want is to pacify my injured soul.

One dip of my baby toe into the pool of euphoria and I'm charmed by the face of fraud. I want to feel like this every day. Starved for protection and unaware of disease, I vow my unending loyalty to the trick of mind that is addiction.

Captive.

5

STAR LIGHT - STAR BRIGHT

Star light, star bright,
The first star I see tonight;
I wish I may, I wish I might,
Have the wish I wish tonight.

Buddy needs to tighten up on his ball skills and the best place for that is in-town. River Park Apartments. Better known as the projects. Like a tame pet I trail close behind, happy to break free from home and the stuffy confines of my own thinker.

The brothers don't give two shits about Buddy or his corny little basketball. There's no distracting them from me. None. He can't get their attention, not if he'd been giving away Bentleys. It's all about Texas.

It's like I've opened the front door to Ed McMahon holding that huge check. But money alone can't afford such pleasure. The *why* is what's best. It's my "bubble-butt" as the boys in gym class chant. "Tex-ass" is loved here.

I've died and gone straight to heaven. I'm sure of it. Held captive by a deep inhale of triumph, I hunger for more. I look like an uncaged ferret—dashing here and there with my pointy little nose into everything.

Back in Melbourne we played House, Truth or Dare, and Spin the Bottle so much that in the end we skip the game part. That's how I first learn of the power held in the hidden bush. With this response I become bold. Unstoppable.

★ ★ ★

Hanging out in brown town is frowned upon, but dating a black guy is unacceptable. So…

…I find me a cute one. Sean Jackson. A nice boy. Gets great grades and he's super funny. He goes to a different school but we find ways to see each other. I keep it a secret because I've seen how cruel kids can be to people of color. Don't care about me. Just don't want anyone to be mean to him.

I go in-town each morning but not to see Sean. To buy three pre-rolled joints and sell them at school. Been smoking everyday for two weeks—since the movie.

The reception I received on my trip with Buddy makes getting reefer effortless. Not only that, when drugs are involved, no one cares where you get them. Anything for a good excuse. I pay a dollar apiece, but charge two bucks with the understanding they'll be smoking with me. My free lunch is sold to Fat-Freddy for tomorrow's gas money.

"Born to hustle." That's what Cali says when he grudgingly opens the door at 6:20 each morning. These words feed my deep hunger for cause.

One morning he opens the door naked and pushes his weed tray into my chest. "I ain't gettin' up at no 6 AM ev'ryday to roll three one dolla' bones for your white-ass."

I stroll past him unaffected. Smiling. I set the tray on the kitchen table and say, "But it's me. You gotta look out for the white-girl."

"I'm gon' look out, aw'ight." He throws a pack of Job rolling papers at me and says, "Today ya learn ta roll. How's dat?" Then back to bed he goes kicking his room door closed.

I glance around in confusion. Don't even know where to start. I grab a banana from atop the refrigerator and a Pepsi from inside. His place is fresh. Furnished in black and gold. Can't believe he just left me out here.

Never do make it to school that day, but I learn to roll. Hours of ridiculous attempts at smoking half-rolled joints gets me high. Cali wakes up. Walks over to the tray and bursts into laughter. "I see you foun' a way to at leas' smoke." Pouring a bowl of frosted flakes he motions for the tray. Then tutors me through the process until I'm an expert.

Arrogance slapped by rejection, doused in shame and pumped fat with rebellion, forms a camaraderie. I like these folks. Pride grows guts and convinces me I belong here. And so without hesitation, in great confidence, I kick off my sandals, prop up my feet, and light a Virginia Slim. Home.

The old railroad tracks run straight through the middle of the projects. On one side stands the Gordon River Apartments, on the other River Park. River Park is where Sean lives. Everyone hangs here in the evenings. After our usual thirty minute, gotta-go/gonna-stay goodbyes, I find the strength to head home. On my way out I run into William King. Billy.

"Haven't I met you before?" I ask.

"Yah, girl, don't you remember? At the Rec, on the other side of the tracks."

I know he sells pot but what I don't realize is The King has sworn to make me his girl. He's popular, so having his attention delights me.

"Hey, Texarkana, how 'bout you come hang at my place for a minute or two?"

His pad is party central. The hotspot. Gotta check it out.

"Okay, I'll be there in a few." I head for my car. Cranking the engine I follow his lead. By the time I walk up he's propped against the hood of his Lincoln. "Let's chill a sec 'n burn a joint firs'," he suggests.

"Why ya wit' Sean? He don't know what ta do with a Queen like you."

"I love him." I respond with a twisted expression. "Why you asking me that? Is that why you invited me here, Billy?"

"Naw, Tex. Come on man, let's go in. They watchin' Scarface."

I like Billy King. A lot. The way he dresses and handles himself. Smooth. He cracks jokes I can tell no one else gets. We have an immediate unspoken bond. Something special. Even after what comes later, I feel no bitterness when I think of him.

Seduced by a strange reverence, I can't drag my eyes from the television screen. I watch with envy as Al Pacino and the other men gawk at Michelle Pfeiffer's ascent in the glass elevator. They're awestruck. A scene I'll never forget.

My mind's made up. Someday I'll be the girl in the glass elevator.

Don't remember my first kiss, first crush, first anything. Not sure why. Could it be I was too young. Maybe I knew it was wrong and ex'd it from my head. However it all went down, I got the gist. Being a girl's like being a soldier. It gives you rank, authority, and a weapon. Exhilarating.

The movie ends. My mind's then free to review my locale. I watch Billy for a minute. Can't seem to help myself. He's charming. A group of people to my right talk and laugh. The excitement of their discussion diverts my attention. They're chatting about a man named Joseph Jackson.

"He da biggest dealer eva hit de's parts." Interested in their intense facial expressions, the wonder of this mysterious man allures me.

By some fateful act I'm sure isn't God, I learn his identity to be my boyfriend's father. Go figure. Without a second breath my main priority becomes to meet Mr. Joseph Jackson.

Sean's dad's a huge drug distributor and pimp. He rose to glory in a small farming area in this county. He's now black-balled from Southwest Florida. Beating a prostitute with a hot clothes iron he swung from the cord. That was the final straw. Didn't stop him. Just picked up shop and relocated to the city. Miami.

I'll need my finely developed art of persuasion if I expect to get Sean's help in this matter. He wants nothing to do with the man. The pain and embarrassment his mother suffered ensures this. No prob. I'm up for the challenge. The lower the odds the bigger the payoff. Isn't that how the gamble goes?

My fear factor's a big fat zero. All I'm concerned with is my passage to the big-time. It's no easy task but eventually I get my wish. Miami here I come.

Escape's a myth. No matter where you run reality follows. Change remains one's sole release and true desire it's only motivator. But how can I fix what I don't know is broken? What

I want forms what I get, and once addicted my wants are polluted.

Fastened to a self-contrived promise of importance I zoom off so fast the world becomes a smudge. Lies take root like a Banyan tree with stems and shoots running every which way. I'm overtaken by absurd beliefs that rise up and choke out sensibility. Circumstance covered in counterfeit possibilities begin to suffocate what's left of rational thought.

Mesmerized.

6

BREAD-N-HONEY

The king was in his counting house,
Counting out his money;
The queen was in the parlor,
Eating bread and honey.
The maid was in the garden,
Hanging up the clothes;
Along came a blackbird,
And pecked off her nose.

Excitement ignites my insides when Sean knocks. Like a movie, the door opens and through the haze Joseph Jackson comes into focus. Dressed in a teal silk, long-sleeve shirt and dark blue, perfectly creased Jordache jeans. The stitch is golden. A flawless blend with his snake-skin boots. The funk of stale cigarettes permeates the room. Smoke's so thick a searchlight couldn't keep me from tripping over the Rottweilers lying inside the door.

My eyes search the room. Mesmerized by the scent of Newports and cognac, I notice an enormous black man behind Mr. Jackson. He wears a gun and watches a collage of TV screens. They picture each angle of the building. Inside and out. To the right there's a wet bar loaded with E&J, Courvoisier and Hennessy. The same stuff the fellas back home drink on Fridays.

On the glass top table there's a shimmering mound of white stuff. Looks like leftovers from a smashed chalk box. Must be cocaine. Beside the heap there's an ace of spades and an assortment of different-sized miniature Ziploc bags. Curious.

Two half-naked girls, with heels as high as church steeples, push past us with their chins in the air. I see them from the edge of my eye but my gaze is fixed on him. The infamous Jo-Jo Jackson. It's been years but Jo-Jo greets his son as if only hours have passed.

"Hey boy, glad ya here. I see ya brought some friends. Y'all gonna have ta wait back there for a minute. Got biniz ta tend to." With an incarcerating stare he leads us across the house to a bedroom. He abruptly closes the door on his way out. The four of us have been in here for 40 minutes. Silently aware we have no rights. Left them at the front door. Like everyone else who enters.

Jo-Jo Jackson is a celebrity in Naples. Can't believe I got Sean to bring me. He was finished with his dad long ago. Hasn't laid eyes on him in three years, and it took me three months to beg him into this trip.

Derrick, Sean, and I do everything together. Samantha makes four. Sammy's the toughest gator to skin but she has a car and a 2 a.m. curfew. I need her. At first, no matter what I say, she's way too scared. Not by the criminal aspect, but her background doesn't allow for the mixing of races. I tell the most intriguing Joseph Jackson stories I know. Doesn't help. In the end, all I need to hitch this ride is the promise of cocaine.

The scene in the bedroom looks like this. The door closes and no one dare open it. Sean's busy. In and out of drawers, boxes, shoes and pockets. Derrick's anxious. He wrings his hands in worry thinking something may go wrong to keep him from a basketball scholarship. Sammy's sick. She sits on the bed with her knees to her chest. Freaked out—practically crying. I'm enthralled. I stand, ear pressed to the door, starved to hear every word spoken in the next room.

I'm right where I want to be. Billy King will be so impressed. Proud. Why do I care what he thinks? I'm doing my thing. I've pushed the Up button and await the glass elevator.

I hear a woman. Must be a girl under that blanket I saw on the couch. She sobs. Jo-Jo's tone is vicious. A slap, a crash, then more crying. That must be one of his whores. She obviously did something wrong.

Never do learn what that is. But I live to see many a busted lip, bruised body or blackened eye. I see missing teeth, welted backs and broken bones. I hear stories of a crushed cheekbone, a hanging eyeball, even a four finger hand. The pinky wore Jo-Jo's stolen ring.

Some things you know better than to believe and some you know better than not to. It's true. I'm sure of it, but my mask of excitement repels caution.

A pushy dude in his late 20s throws open the bedroom door. Almost knocks me over. "Come out," he says in a smart-ass tone. The missing hump on the couch leaves question. What happened out here?

"These bitches'll make ya hafta kill 'um," Jo-Jo says with a careless shrug.

Three new guys have joined the room. I'm certain by their obedient expressions they work for him. He hands them each a brown sack. Strange thing. On their way out, they stuff them down the front of their pants. No idea what that's about.

"Sorry y'all had ta hear that shit but that's how 'dis game go." He motions us to join him at the table. Memory looses sight with time, leaving me unclear on the whereabouts of Sean and Derrick. Sammy and I? We sit like trained animals. I take the closest seat, of course. The white pile of coke is much smaller and the mini-bags are scattered between oceans of money. You only see this type of stuff on TV. Some FBI sting documentary or something.

He pulls some powder away from the lumps and straightens it out with a card. Fanning a stack of money on the table he pushes a hundred dollar bill in my direction.

"Roll dat up white-gurl and getcha a toot," he says with a gleaming gold-tooth grin. Then slaps the card down on the table and puts both hands behind his shiny, perfectly arranged, Jheri-Kurls. "I use an ace of spades when baggin' my product. Brings luck and ya need plenty of dat in dis worl'. It's part of my stay-out-of-jail formula," he says with a childlike smirk. "Don't wanta hav'ta use a get-out-of-jail card—even if it is free. Much better ta not get got in da firs place."

Hypnotized. Like an eighth-grader watching her favorite rock star I can hardly speak. I open my mouth to say no thanks when under the table Sammy's knee to my thigh says different. Once my senses find me, I remember my half-cocked promise to get her high.

"Sure," comes my reply. And with the anxious cheer of a job applicant I roll the bill for Sam to use as a straw. Suddenly I notice Sean. It's like he appeared in some street corner magic act. His face is what keeps me from sniffing some up myself.

The Virginia Slims I smoke don't bother him but he says, "Girls on cocaine are capable of anything." I make eye contact with him. He taps his watch. It's getting late. How disappointing. Too much time in the bedroom.

Although he keeps a close eye on me, Sean is distracted with the surveillance cameras. He, Derrick and the gunman joke as they watch a couple in the alley doing god knows what. Jo-Jo takes the opportunity to scoop up some cocaine and pour it into a baggy.

"It's mine if it got dollar signs on it. Only I got access to des bad boys." With lips puckered, he nods his chin in my direction. Looking down I notice the green dollar signs printed on each bag.

It seems like everyone in the room stands when he stands. On our way to the door he leans over and kisses my head, pushing the little bag into my pocket. I feel special. The last one out the door, I look up at him.

"You need this, sugah'?" he asks and with a green-eyed wink he slips me the rolled bill.

★ ★ ★

Outside the city we stop at 7-11. Need fuel. Sam and I scurry to the bathroom. I pull the bag from my pocket. It doesn't look like much but when I show Samantha she starts dancing. "This has to be two grams, Texas. He gave you two grams, two whole grams. Yes! Way to go."

The flash of her smile brightens the drab room. Cocaine's power brought her here even though she was scared to death. This reaction is my first glance at the force of this mysterious powder.

She shakes a few clumps out, carefully zips the bag and pushes it into her bra. Then out comes a razor from what looks like a sewing kit she caries in her purse. After a smash or two and a dozen chops, she turns to hand me a straw. Like

59

an aristocrat: I raise my hand, cross my leg, and bow. My right hand presenting the other surprise.

"The hundred?" she shrieks. "He gave you this too?"

With smiles stuccoed to our faces we hold hands and laugh. All around the neglected restroom we jump. Up-and-down, up-and-down. As if we'd won a week's stay at the Ritz Carlton.

I lean forward and Sammy holds my hair back. I suck up my first line of cocaine off the back of a broken toilet, through a dirty hundred dollar bill.

The trip's a life changer. For the last five hours I've been linking together a warped puzzle. Once completed, I'm captivated by it's wonder. Intoxicated by narcotics, exhilaration breathes life to dreams of lunacy too detailed to describe. I foster these reckless lies as my own, deliberate to nurture them until they are fully grown.

Belted to the cockpit by falsehood, intentions take flight. Fantasy overpowers integrity. I'm launched into an unrehearsed free fall. No concern for my own safety and too excited for common sense.

Buzzed.

7

FAST AS YOU CAN

Run, run as fast as you can!
You can't catch me. I'm the Gingerbread Man!

1:25 a.m. That's what my watch reads when we hit Naples. The trip across Alligator Alley to meet Mr. Jackson was terrifically mind-blowing. Even today, as I write, a bubbling sensation scuttles throughout my stomach. Like a child on her first trip to Disney. Can't wait to tell Billy King.

Sam and I rush to the projects to drop off the guys, then head to her house. The line of cocaine I did at the gas station caused a chemical smell in my nose and my mouth still tastes of medicine. Now it seems part of my face has been erased. Up all night doing lines. Other than sleepless, I don't feel very buzzed. Certainly nothing I can't live without.

I make it home about 8 o'clock Saturday evening. Haven't heard from Sean. Must be the trip. I wonder if his mom caught him coming in late. At 9 or so the next evening I hear a tap on my bedroom window. I push back the curtain to Derrick's worried expression.

"Dey got Sean," he says.

"Who got Sean?"

"The po'leece. Dey got him. The gun jus went off. He didn't mean to. He's gone."

"What the hell are you talking about?" I shout.

"Shh," Derrick whispers.

"The last thing I need is your big, white daddy finding my black-ass at your window. Here's what happened. At his dad's, Sean found a gun. Sammy was too scared ta notice and you was busy listenin' at da door. Sean hid it in his jacket. At the community center the next day, Sean went ta showin' it off to da fellas. It accidentally went off and shot Mick in da leg. He's okay but at da hospital. Dey took Sean to juvie hall. The gun's got two bodies on it and who knows what else. Sean's in trouble, Tee. Real trouble."

"What? It was used in two murders?" I begin to cry.

How can this be true? It's all my fault.

To dismiss blame I attempt to fix things. I call Sean's mom. She agrees to take me to the center to visit him the next night. I apologize to Ms. Sug over and over. She matter-of-factly assures me it's not my fault. "Sean know better than to have a gun, gurl. Don't blame ya'self."

I'm used to hanging in Gordon River a couple of nights a week. Weekends too. With Sean gone I get in the habit of chillin' at Billy's crib. Wish we were together but he's got a girl. He's always telling me how much he likes me when she's not around. All that does is make me wonder if he can be trusted. Doubtful.

In my worthless effort to get over what happened, I decide I'm done with Naples. Sean's locked-up, Billy's busy, and I've been incarcerated by the illusion of infamy. The rich better-than-me's and cool know-it-all's blur what's left of my vision. My hunger for the unfamiliar leaves me with no taste for the ordinary. Life in Miami would be far better than the insignificant one I have here.

With both hands reaching forward I cling to the notion of candy kisses and gumdrops—certain only a fool would not. I won't be held hostage any longer. Besides, I must warn Jo-Jo the police have that gun.

I look around but have no idea who will take me. As a last resort I decide to ask Nikki. She's not someone I hang with but she dates black guys and hates this town. She agrees. And so I leave home at the age of seventeen on a mission to become authentic and find out the truth. The one that's been concealed from me.

Prince is screaming from the speakers in the trunk when Nicki pulls her avocado-colored Dodge Charger into the driveway. "Turn that down. Don't need the neighbors watching," I say as I heave my bags into the trunk. My parents are always paying attention to those in crisis, no clue what's going on with me. They want crisis? I'll show them crisis. With as little regard as a chick leaving it's broken shell, I'm off to discover the real world.

"Derrick's coming too," I inform.

Derrick lives a few blocks from me and rides my bus. He plays on the basketball team with Buddy. We're both Juniors. After my first trip to the projects we become friends. He introduced me to Sean. They're best buds. This was six months back but feels like a lifetime. My view of the world is different now—to say the least.

Barely a friend, still the facts are clear. Nikki's life's been submerged in injustice. Rejected, abused, judged and abandoned.

I feel for her. She only dates blacks—a "nigger lover." Everybody knows that. Me dating Sean gives us common ground. She's the perfect choice for my mission. Can't move to Miami and live with Jo-Jo with no ride or knowledge of African Americans. I need transportation as well as a life-map if I hope to navigate my way through this maze. Nicki offers both. Like a Lamborghini, I rocket from 0 to 90 in next to nothing.

Don't suppose I'll ever forget my inflated ego the day we arrive—all belongings in tow. It takes us a bit to locate Mr. Jackson. He rarely stays in the same place. Joseph opens the door to the apartment with an almost electric grin. I swear I can see his molars.

"Mr. Jackson I had to come and warn you. They arrested Sean with a gun he stole from the Big House."

"I already know dis," he says with a wink. He turns to the trashy, over-decorated girls on the couch. "Y'all hard-headed bitches better listen up. As long as I live, anythin' I got, dis girl right here can get. She's mo' loyal to me than any of y'all stankin-ass hoes."

He leads us to a back room. For hours I sit on the edge of the bed listening intently to his every word. He's high. I come to learn the expression on his face when he gets like this. If Jo-Jo's been up for too long his left eye wanders while the other stares at you. Eerie at first but as our relationship grows I begin to poke-fun. I'm brave like that and he loves it.

Within a week Nicki's got a new name. Lyric. She's on the hoe stroll. A prostitute. Can't believe she'd do that. Not me. Jo-Jo has thirty-six children (no joke). Sean's his favorite. This gives me privilege. "A powder-head hoe or hustler can't be trusted," Jo-Jo cautions. I'm proud to be the only member of the crew allowed to snort. Definite perk.

★ ★ ★

The Family Restaurant is on the corner of 23rd St. and Biscayne Blvd. Jo-Jo owns it. One evening I go in to order some fried fish and hush puppies. Only been waiting a minute but the two men that walked in behind me are cops. Guaranteed. Jo-Jo has them down pat and he taught me how to spot them.

"Dey wear brand-new white sneakers. Clean as a virgin. And dark blue jeans. You'll know dey don't belong. Jus will." Jo-Jo knows the cops are looking for me. He always knows everything.

I walk from the restaurant towards the house. I'll send somebody else to get my food. Just in case. When I walk out they follow. "Texas? Texas Poulsen. Wait a minute Ms. Poulsen. Stop! We're Miami Vice." I ditch my sandals and take off running. They're big guys but that doesn't keep them from catching up. They wrestle me to the ground and cart me to the precinct.

"Your dad will be here soon."

Then come the questions.

"I have no idea what you're talking about," I say. "I swear, never heard of anybody by that name." They flip to a picture of me driving the Corvette. Joseph's in the front seat. For what seems like forever, stories are told, videos shown. All in attempts to reveal to me the seriousness of this situation.

Don't remember a word spoken. That's how interested I am. There is no changing my mind. Dead to emotion I watch the room as if looking down on it. I'm shielded from concern. Held hostage in a tower I built—lie upon lie. I'm relieved not to care. Cared too much for too long, I figure.

Can't even describe my father's expression or attitude. It doesn't matter how he feels. His years of so-called protection have achieved nothing. He can drive me home as many times as he wants, I'll be eighteen in less than four months. Then what?

The hushed ride home seems like an eternity. Miserable. No shoes and I'm a mess from my struggle with the detectives. I can see the heartsick alarm in Dad's eyes. I'm sure he's already passed judgment. He thinks they found me like this. No way. He just doesn't realize I have it made here.

The following week I'm guarded as if I have access to an atomic bomb. When tensions relax, I'm able to escape two more times. Once I hitchhike all the way to Miami. I'm found two weeks later, hauled back, and taken through various exercises in hopes of exorcising my demons.

My dad finally gives up. At work he gets word I'm taking off again. Dismay and grief escort him to the school. He pulls up the exact moment I'm on my way out the front door. "Texas, I'm not going to stop you again. Is this what you really want?"

My response is hardened. Unaffected by his tears. "This is what I have to do, Dad."

Gone.

8

JIGGITY-JIG

To market, to market, to buy a fat pig,
Home again, home again, jiggety-jig.
To market, to market, to buy a fat hog,
Home again, home again, jiggety-jog.

"You pic' Tex. Jus' pick. Switch it up in a few weeks if you want." A tan Cadillac Eldorado, a mint-green Porsche 944, a Greenwood Edition Corvette—black with gold accents. A stolen car ring out of Michigan provides new cars every six to eight weeks.

"Dat keeps 'em guessin'," Jo-Jo says.

"Who guessing?" I ask.

"Da hol' worl'. Dat's who. Da cops, da robbers, da slobs dat slobber. Whoeva watchin'."

My favorite is the white Biarrtiz Cadillac. A convertible with red leather interior. I keep it for two months until the heat it draws starts to make me nervous. Driving around in a stolen car with a three thousand dollar package of cocaine in your lap gets spooky. But caution's gone. MIA.

Jo-Jo's not his usual self. He moved to the outskirts of a neighboring town last week. A trailer. Not a bad spot but not like the big house. Morning and evening I deliver merchandise from one county to the next. My pay is three and one-half grams (an eight ball). Love this job. Mainly because of the drugs but the cars ain't bad either.

I pull over on at least one of my daily trips. You know the median on the interstate? The place where cops wait to catch speeders. That's where. "Da more ridiculous, da less obvious." Heard that rule twenty times this month.

Bought a little red stapler. It's exactly like the one Jo-Jo uses to fastened the filled bags. "Dis keep da wise guys out," he informs. "Don't won' no body stealin' my profit. Gotta be wiser than da wise guys."

After removing the staples I flick them from the car window. Gotta be careful. Jo-Jo notices everything. I open the Ziplocs taking a little scoop from the ones that are over a gram. Tricky. This stunt could get me beaten or killed. I'm not scared. Get high enough and logic is lost. Snorting an average of eight grams a day. Still the itch for more remains unscratched.

Cocaine gives a ridiculous sense of invincibility. Selling or using. Thank goodness for the power of my parent's prayers. No doubt it saved my life. Many times over.

Joseph loves to rehearse rules. "School-ya," he calls it. I learn more in my nine months with him than I do the remainder of my 28 year drug run. My belief in his way leaves me unable to accept different. He's an observant instructor who loves power and attention. I'm a hungry student eager to devour each word. Wonder how this story would have ended had I not spent this time under his direction. Not good. That's sure.

One of the Big Man's rules for me is that I must bring food with me to eat in front of him before my morning re-up.

"Don't want no poor, scrawny lookin' bitches 'round me. Not here, not now, not ever. Got it, White-gurl?"

Many of the whores are white. One day I blurt out the question. "Why do you call *me*, white-girl?"

"You special, that's why. White-gurl."

My entire life I waited to hear these words. They quench rejection's flame and guarantee my commitment to his cause. "Y'za Massa," I say, with my usual glow of adoration. He laughs and continues working.

I feed Bonnie and Clyde (the Rottweilers) my sausage links under the table. I can handle grits but the spicy sausage doesn't mix well with an acidy stomach. He never notices. The newly mastered art of cooking freebase has his undivided attention.

Anger towards authority leaves me blind to the need for guidelines. I can only see things from my absurd mountain of masquerades. A despicable place for a seventeen year old to leap from. Indulgent pleasure can reroute even an attentive conscience. My life's descending fast. No landing strip in sight.

The cops are honing in on the organization. We all know it. Jo-Jo's angry. A lot. High more than usual. He sent many of the girls packing. I'm gone from the hotel. Moved in with the bunch of them. Wild. They abandoned the Big House and came out here. He keeps threatening to haul ass. Go to North Carolina.

Why does he stay? Freebase, that's why. It's selling like hot cakes. I make three and four trips a day to drop off packages. Locked trunks of money are stacked everywhere. Can't believe Ebony, Lyric, and him can move in that bedroom. There's hardly an inch of floor space.

One afternoon as I sit waiting on a full delivery pouch, I hear a noise outside the trailer door. I tap Joseph's hand and point in that direction. The bright silver knob begins to shuffle. Seems weak—like most trailer's—but four additional bolts and a chain hold it tight. Violent knocks come next. Vibration forces a huge ceramic cross, that holds a very dead Jesus from the paneled wall, straight to the floor. The dogs go crazy. Barking and panting. We're silent, all thinking the same thing. Beyond the stillness I hear a familiar voice.

"Open dis door. I ain't da' po'leece."

It's Sean. Defiance rises as excuses hurdle from the right to the left side of my skull. Been a long time. I used to like him so much but nothing's the same anymore. I'm sure he's here to rescue me but I don't need saving. I'm good.

"Somebody get da damn door. That's my boy. He's a free bird." Jo-Jo shouts.

It's not a pleasant encounter but my brain is bare of specifics. Amazing what your mind will and won't remember. Sean leaves within the hour, hurt and confused. I do remember that.

My delivery ride to the city is packed with thoughts of wonder. What if he's right? Is my brain trashed? Doesn't matter. Why'd he bother coming anyway?

Morning breaks and I'm still awake. Cocaine. I wipe my nose. Jo-Jo walks in to the kitchen table, wrinkled brow apparent. He pinches his chin between his thumb and pointer. No wink for me today. I know what's coming. My troubled expression forces his hand to my shoulder and his face takes on a soft expression. Like a charmer woos a snake he speaks in a rhythmic manner. My body sways back-and-forth, entranced by each melodious word.

"Ya know I love you, gurl, right?" he says, smile glowing like a Christmas ornament. "The heat's on. It ain't on-a-count a you. It's jus dis ain't no place to be, baby. Not now. I couldn't live with myself if you go down on-a-count of me. I'm gonna hook ya up with a lil somthin'-somthin'. Then ya gotta make your own way, White-gurl."

My eyes grow warm with sorrow. He's right. Funny things have been happening. Yesterday a cable man came. Said he was here to run cable that no one ordered. Strange cars with dark tint sit down the street at the Dead End sign. Weird.

Joseph's nervous. He went nuts two days ago and beat Rapper senseless thinking he was wearing a wire—ended up a pack of Kools. Not a good scene.

Where will I go? Don't know but I'll be ok. I have the rules memorized. They repeat in my head at night like a vinyl album with a scratch.

"If it don't make dollars, it don't make sense."

"All ya got in life is ya word, so do what ya say."

"There's nothin' ya can't get wit a stack of money or a sack a cocaine. Keep both."

The one that proves most valuable is this one. "Lessin' you a trick—and you ain't no trick—da promise of sex is far mo valuable than da sex itself. Give it away too easy and it won't be worth a dusty dime."

Wiping my wet cheeks, I drop into his favorite recliner like a load of wet laundry.

"Never lose heart, White-gurl. Not eva. You can have it all. Ya hear? You a grade A, bad bitch. Don't you forget dat."

Later that afternoon Rapper takes me to the bus station. And with five hundred bucks and an ounce of the finest cocaine

I jump on the west bound Greyhound. Can't wait to see Billy. To tell The King all I've learned. Maybe he's single now.

Next stop, Naples Projects.

Fame.

9

ASHES, ASHES

Ring-a-around-the-rosies,
A pocket full of posies;
Ashes! Ashes!
We all fall down.

ighteen feels old when you're eighteen. It's the late 80s. Whitney Houston is saving all her love while drugs are stealing all mine. Things were easier in Miami. I miss my role there. It required far less sacrifice. All it took to stay high was to do what I was told.

Naples is an odd place. Not like the city. It's taken longer for the civil rights movement to slow down and settle in. White girls are shunned by their own for going to a place like this. Me? I live here. The projects. There's no embarrassment due to my change in company. Love the fame. Actually, I'm sure I'll be the person to overcome the stereotype. I'm the one still moving. And much too fast.

I'm beat. It's Thursday morning and I need sleep. Bad. Friday's a blink away. Can't afford to be tired on the hottest day of the week. Yes, it's Florida but I'm not referring to the mercury. Everybody spends on Big Money Friday.

I finish my joint and flick the roach. "See you guys tomorrow. I'm gone."

I round the corner headed for home. Billy King's place. Headquarters. Location is everything. Thought I'd be okay here but it bothers me. He's dating my best friend, Alexandra. I know in my heart how he feels about me but he's too proud to take the risk. Scared I won't slow down for him. He's probably right. The three of us live together in his dad's old house. I even have my own room.

Billy was away at college on a full baseball scholarship a few years prior. A dream-killing knee injury brought his future to a howling halt. This sadness, along with the death of his beloved father, devastated him. Not sure which loss hit the black community harder in our small, semi-segregated town.

Deception's disguise is clever. It creates a mirage. The image of a high-roller revives Billy's hope. The next best thing to MLB. The attention I've acquired places me on the same hot air balloon. Extravagant plans and dreams are certain to fill what's empty, or at least distract from loss. I myself am fully devoted to any plan other than the one the church offers.

All or nothing. That's how I play—so all it is.

The sky is starless. A deep navy. The sour smell of brackish water floats up from the river. In the quiet, from behind the stairwell, I hear a familiar voice.

"Hey, Tomcat. Look here."

"Racket, is that you?" I reply. "Are you ok?"

His face wears the rude reflection of panic, brought on by too much coke. He's wired. The closer I get the bigger his eyes grow, like a deer who's spotted the huntsman.

I follow in silence as he climbs the concrete steps to his place. He forces open the door to his dumpster-furnished apartment. Strange smell. Not the usual mildewy mix of recycled cigarettes and warmed-over green beans. Instead it's sweet. A little tart even. Only been here a few times. Not exactly my scene. I flip the switch. No glow follows.

"Did Florida Power close you down?" I joke.

Without the slightest smile he says, "Been waitin' on you, Tex. Knew ya'd be bendin' dat corner sooner or later."

Racket is an older black man. Fiftyish. Nice guy, considering. He's what the girls call a good paymaster. His dad headlined for a big name band in the 50s. Daddy's death affords him the meaty check he's awarded each month. Rack likes the ladies and is free-hearted with the candy. Not a man who's short on company. Good thing. Helps him keep his hands to himself. I don't put up with that crap from men. Not yet anyway.

The Sex Factor makes this life a cinch. No matter how many No's they hear, it seems men don't get it. Learned that way before high school. Somewhere in their tiny overstimulated brains, fantasy hangs tight. Their hunger gives me power and I learn to use it well.

Without hesitation I head towards the flicker of a candle in the back room. I'm a white girl. No black man in his right mind wants to deal with the trouble I can bring. I'm safe.

I shuffle past a grave-yard of empty beer cans, busted dishes, and miscellaneous stiff clothing. The bedsprings complain as I plop down on the yellowed mattress. The reek of urine and musty shoes can't overtake this new odor. Unsure of the source, I scan the room for the usual paraphernalia.

"Where's the straw and plate," I question.

"Not today," Racket insists. He reaches behind a battered sheet that's carelessly tacked over the window and from the ledge he pulls a mangled Old Milwaukee can.

Puzzled, I shrug. "What's that?"

"This, Darlin', will rock your world," he says and points the sideways crumpled can in my direction. "Jus listen to me, Tex, and do what I say. Dis'll take you to a place you'll neva wanna leave."

If I knew then what I now know, would I have chosen to board this aircraft? Would I have taken the trip? I'd like to think not. If I realized the outrageous cost I'd pay with my very soul, would I have gone home to my family then? Who knows? Too late for what-ifs now. I grab the can.

"Easy with dat, girl. It's you pipe. This is cooked cocaine. Freebase dey call it—ya smoke it." Racket hands me a hard beige chunk. I place it on the can as instructed. It looks like a Jaw Breaker you've sucked for ten minutes, or something you plucked from the seashore. I cradle the can in my palm, balancing the freebase rock atop the ash Rack dumped on it.

"Give me dat lighter, gurl. I'll turn it on for ya. You jus' pull. Slow—till da rock melts."

A pearly taste coats my throat. He raises his hand like a stop sign and I move my mouth from the can. Heavy smoke curls upward. "Perfect. Now… let out all da air from your chest before ya pull in da smoke. See ya when ya get back," he says with a dirty-toothed grin."

The fire glows. I draw in—strong and steady.

"Pull as hard as ya can white-gurl. Good, I can tell, ya gettin' it." Smoke slips from the edge of my mouth. "Don't let any out, gurl. Is you crazy? That was a huge hit and it's your firs' one. De'll neva be anotha' like it. Hold it, Tomcat."

I can feel the color leave my face from lack of oxygen, but I don't dare breathe. Racket reaches over and rubs my thigh. "Man! You a fine-ass white-gurl." I push his hand away and stand. I tilt my head back and let the smoke rush from my lungs.

Waves of toasty sensations pulse through me. Side-to-side I sway, like Hansel and Gretel leaving breadcrumbs. Unfamiliar pleasure rocks me, as if standing in the center of a cheering arena. Only sound's half muted. My throat seems blocked by unexpected excitement.

Small lights flash. Sorta like the test at the eye doctor's office. Problem is, I can't stay focused enough to keep track. Thoughts spin beyond my intelligence. Energy flutters like a bird against my rib cage. Colors are bright. Then I'm blinded by a warm and comfortable darkness. Consumed. Full force. It's fabulous.

Then as fast as it comes it goes. Leaving a gap the size of Texas in my chest, or maybe it's all in my mind. Don't know. To be honest, don't care either.

"Wow, man. Wow! What else do you say to that? Wow!"

Don't remember sitting back down. Words wander in and out of my skull like a violated ant hill. I lay back for a minute and as if spoken in trance I mumble. "Let me get another, Rack?"

This new little goody leaves zero room for distraction. Strangled by lust and soaked in greed, I watch his every move. Stunned and determined. Without reservation I go for round two. Next comes three. Three plus three makes 33. Add three more and it's 333. And so it goes. Bound without chains. I miss Big Money Friday. Saturday too. The term out-of-control gains sharp clarity.

The washhouse is where most business transactions take place. My role there is important to me. This behavior's unheard of. After smoking his $500 worth, I let him cook up more and more cocaine until my stash is gone. I even spend my re-up money. Billy's gonna kill me.

The high gobbles up time. No sleep or food. Nothing to drink but beer for fifty-two hours. Don't even like beer. Finally, with no possibility for more, the thin light of Monday creeps through the open window urging me home. I stagger toward Billy's before night's curtain lifts, exposing me—dirty, hungry, and broke.

The projects surge with fresh enthusiasm. Hurry, hurry, hurry, step right up. Climb aboard the base rock express. Everyone's taking freebase for a test drive. Why not? Smart dealers are quick to offer samples. One hit guarantees big business. The non-addict slams on the breaks after the first round, while the addict rushes right past the blinking hazards. Top speed.

Pride. A cunning enemy of freedom. I see others losing control but swear it won't happen to me. I'm not smoking that junk again. Never. Not ever. It's not for me.

Messy.

10

SHUT THE DOOR

One, two,
Buckle my shoe;
Three, four,
Shut the door;
Five, six,
Pick up sticks;
Seven, eight,
Lay them straight:
Nine, ten,
A big, fat hen.

My work's cut out for me. Gotta do some serious hustling to get on my feet. My weekend smoking adventure knocked me down a few notches. Billy's not mad. I told him the truth. He shook his head and called me a dumb-ass.

"Don't mess around with dat freebase. I'm warnin' you gurl. What you need is a real man. No tellin' wat'll end-up happenin' wit you, Texarkana. You a hardhead." The screen door slams behind him. He walks along the sidewalk towards his car, banging his forehead as if I'm dense.

Disappointed in myself. A messy situation. Hate letting Billy down. No druggin' for me for a piece. Gotta pull my purse strings together. Get back on my mission. I'll get my paper straight. Don't you worry 'bout that.

Awake by 10 a.m.—out till 4 a.m. Five days and I'm back in the groove. No debt, product in hand. Eight days and I'm ahead. Thank god, I miss my partner-in-crime—cocaine. It's been hard staying up all night without her.

My eyes open Saturday by noon and before I even use the bathroom I chop out a huge line. Where you been, girl? I wink at the little bag. Hated being without you. I pull a straw off the top of a picture frame that hangs above the glass night stand. With one long snort the powder disappears as if discovered on the dashboard by a car-vac.

I lean my head back, take a long hard sniff, and toss the straw towards the dresser. James Brown invades my brain and so I sing. "I feel good, nana-nana-nana-na. Like I knew that I would, nana-nana-nana na." Now that's what I call a wakeup.

I drop to the bed in the wee hours of Sunday morning. God only knows what drugs I ingested. I'm coherent but in no shape to struggle with a shower. I wiggle out of my jeans and pull on my night clothes. I sigh. Relieved to lay down and be able to breathe freely. My jeans are way too tight. Gotta be sexy—always sexy.

The door hinges creak and light from the hallway shines across my face.

"Who's that?" I say

"Chill, Tee. It's jus me," comes Billy's reply. Nervous curiosity relaxes. I sit forward and prop my pillow against the wall. He sits on the edge of the bed and asks, "Wha'd you get into ta-nite?"

I start laughing and proceed to tell him how Alex got robbed of a $300.00 pack and Miss Roxy got so high she hid behind J building for an hour. He laughs a bit, but not in his usual cheerful way. Odd.

"What's going on Billy." I ask. "Everything good? Why you in here, anyway?"

"Scoot ova, Texas. And lay down. It's all gud."

"Hell no, what are you doing, Billy? You're not the king of this," comes my reply.

"Shh, I'm stayin' in here with you tonight," he reports with matter of fact insistency.

"Bye, Asshole! You got your own room. Lay there." I push his butt with my foot and lay my pillow back down. Grabbing my shoulder he presses me to the mattress. Shocked. This transformation of attitude has me puzzled. Speechless.

"Dat's what you don't seem ta get, gurl. Dis my room too."

Scared to scream, I speak the only words I can come up with. "Where's Alex," I ask. As if caught in a distasteful prank. With one sharp move he parts my knees capturing me by the weight of his body. His cold salty hand covers my mouth, pinning my head to the bed. I pull and shift under the weight of his chest. Trapped. Like a mouse who happened along the wrong piece of cheese.

With his free hand he rips my night-shorts to the side permitting entrance. His speech is calloused sending a thousand needles down my spine. The air is stifling. Horrified. I try to kick.

"Knock it off, Tex. Don't play wit' me. Not ta'nite gurl. You know you want me."

His words swirl and swoop through the air like vultures who've discovered a rotting carcass. Seen Billy angry many times with many people, and though his face is grayed out by darkness, I can feel the crazy in his stare. I could get free from him. I think. But I don't dare.

Questions swarm my skull. How can he do this? I thought he cared? Then I think of the games I've played. He's told me many times he loves me. I pay him no mind. Traveling from Miami to Tampa. Staying in elaborate hotels with various men. I know he thinks I sleep with them but Jo-Jo's right, the possibility of sex is a capable tool.

It's my own fault. I shouldn't be using him and taunting him. Living in his house, doing his drugs. I even slept with his best friend.

I'm still as it happens. Tears fill my ears. They spill onto the sheets beneath me. He's big and it hurts, but not nearly as bad as the blade that gouges in and out of my diluted heart. Release comes as he collapses with a loud exhale onto the bed beside me. I roll from beneath his lifeless leg, collect my jeans, and head to the restroom.

I notice his bedroom door. It's shut. Alex is in there asleep. I push the bathroom door closed and lock it. Grabbing a towel I wipe franticly at my sticky thighs. I plop to the toilet. My chest heaves and tears splash onto my trembling bare legs.

I hear his room door open. Is that him going in, or her coming out? Bombarded with the reality that this could leave me with nowhere to live and no way to stay high, I inhale.

Pull yourself together, Texas. It's over now.

Back in the dark room I'm crowded by sorrow. I fight the tears but they win. Tear after tear. Crushed. Part of me's dying. I can feel it. Everything I thought was different about this world is the same. Using people to get what you want. That's how it goes. I don't matter here either.

I hold the pillow to my face. Don't want to feel the river running down my neck. I cry and cry. Until I'm dry. Dry. Inside and out.

"Shudn't go swallowin' pills you can't handle." That's what I heard at the washhouse last night. I'm the one who took this pill. Gotta find a way to handle it.

★ ★ ★

"What's wrong, Texas?" Alex is in the hallway the next day when I wake.

"Nothing. Why?" She leans in and touches my cheek.

"Your eyes are puffy. There are marks on your neck. You get in a fight or something? What happened?"

I rub my face, run my hands through my hair, and continue gathering my morning supplies. "No fight. I'm fine, girl. Just miss my brother, Curtis. That's all," I say tying on a tired smile.

She stares at me with a sad expression. "Don't lie. You can tell me." I shrug my shoulders and walk from the room. I close the door behind me, leaving last night's memory there. Confined.

"I'll be fine, Allie girl. Don't worry 'bout me. Where's Billy?"

The Rolodex in my mind spins in search of the proper Jo-Jo rule. "If you don't know, jus act like it." It's the only one that shows up. I don't know how this happened, so I'll act like it didn't. That might work.

I pretend everything is as it was. Pretend—until it doesn't matter. But it does matter. It matters a lot. Nothing makes sense anymore. My new belief system's been shot clean through. It's ridiculous. As lame as the setup the church tried to stuff down my throat. Sickening.

Once closed to proper instruction I'm left to form my own wounded theories. In life there's no rewind button. Newton's law of motion is correct. A body in motion does indeed stay in motion and I've been headed in this direction for a good while now.

Being here's no better than being there. Life sucks either way. Maybe I'll go home. Yeah, that's what I'll do. Go home. Until then I should just be easy. Better not confront Billy. Don't want an explosion or anything. Gotta keep my mouth shut.

Tight.

11

LEAVE THEM ALONE

Little Bo Peep
Has lost her sheep,
And doesn't know where to find them.
Leave them alone
And they will come home,
Wagging their tails behind them.

The joke's on me. Things are out of control. This isn't a good life. It's not. I've tried to stop, handle things, keep a decent reputation, but I'm losing it. All of it. I miss my family. They're hurt and it's my fault. Seems easier to stay high then to try to undo what's been done. But high's only temporary.

Disgust with Billy demands change and lack of alternative drives me home. I say whatever I must to make that happen. I want different but don't want to go without. Drugs that is. Within weeks of being home I locate Jo-Jo. He's in South Carolina. A friend of a friend of a friend and ten phone calls later…I'm on my way to the airport. My parents are at church, so I steal a car that's been left at their house.

My note reads: "The car will be at the Fort Myers airport with the keys under the mat. Sorry. Can't do this. I'll call soon. Texas"

Higher and higher the plane climbs causing the buildings below to transform from houses to a Lego village, then a Monopoly board. When the plane lands I grab my bag and hurry outside, anxious to discover what fancy car is waiting to chauffeur me into the mountains.

An older black man in a beat-around pickup is what I find. I don't know him and he's not real friendly. The ride's quiet. Twenty-five long minutes before he pulls up to a rundown motel on the backside of a graveyard.

"What's this?" I ask.

"Dis where ya stayin'. Don' worry dis plac' tight." He pulls around back and hands me a loose key. "Da room dat-a-way." I hoist my duffel bag from the floorboard and the truck's in reverse before my left foot hits the dirt.

The air is fresh, the colors warm, and through recall's door they escort the joys of childhood. But those memories hold no luster compared to his glory. Jo-Jo Jackson. He'll be here soon. Can't wait to see him.

I wait and I wait. The phone isn't turned on and I have no money, so I wait. Sleep apprehends me during a late night episode of Taxi. A light rap on the door wakes me from a discontented sleep. Cheer floods my belly as I leap from the bed.

"Hold-up, I'm coming," I shriek like a child who's heard hooves on the roof Christmas morning. I throw open the door—not to my expected hero—instead the man from yesterday stands before me. Wrinkled brown pants, mis-buttoned flannel, and a fifty in hand.

"Here gurl. Jos'ef? He be thru lata'," he announces as he walks away. Jumping into the worn pickup, he rattles his way down the dusty, uneven drive. I stand frozen. Surprised. Eyes wide with shock, face long with disappointment—crumpled $50 in fist. Jo-Jo must be real busy. He'd never leave me here like this. Not me.

★ ★ ★

Days pass between visits. It's afternoon. I ran out of money yesterday about this time. I'm hungry, no cigarettes, and haven't had a single drug since I exited the plane. Not liking this deal.

The room's billed to a Gold MasterCard. No worries there. That is, if the person on the card really exists. I've become friends with the maids and the dude in the office. But still don't know the man's name who brought me here.

It's fall. The air is cool and clean. Gorgeous. My door's propped open. It's stuffy in here but I don't dare go for a walk. Can't miss the man in the truck when he comes. If he comes. Today, the two of us gotta have a little chat.

The shocks squeak as the ancient pickup thumps into park. The driver's door moans announcing his approach. I roll on my bubble gum lip gloss and lay back attempting to look needy or desirable. Whichever works.

His large shadow crosses the threshold before he reaches my doorway. The sun's behind him and his dark skin makes it impossible to see his facial expression. I smile and with the warmest welcome I can muster, I say, "Thank goodness you're here. I knew you'd come. Come on in. I'm sick of being alone."

Entering, he sits at the half-sized formica table. It's beyond the rickety A/C unit that's halfway mounted in the loose, aluminum window frame. Raggedy. I climb from the bed, pull a chair close to his, and touch his thigh. I hold his stare. "What's your name?"

"Dey call me, Hide, cuzin' I can fine an'body. Can't nobody hide from Hide."

I laugh. "Well, I'm gonna call you Hi-Dad. That alright? Since you're the one taking care of me."

"I ain't the one. Not me. But that don' matta none. I'll answa ta an'thin ya holler. You Texy, rite?"

I giggle and repeat. "Texy? Texy and Hi-Dad. Sounds like quite a team, wouldn't you say?" I burst into laughter and to my surprise he joins me.

"When will Jo-Jo be coming, Hi-Dad? You know?" I ask eyes filled with purposeful twinkle.

He raises his eyebrows. "Oh, he be comin'. Ya kno how he is. E'll come. Not 'for day in da mornin' but when he good-n-ready, dat's when. And not a da' soona, eitha. He tol' me ta ask what ya needin'. I'll get it Texy, don't ya be worrin' nun. Ya wan' it, Hide'll get it."

"Good. My habit's screaming at me, man. That's what I need most." I explain how twelve days have passed with no coke. He stands, smiles, and through his scattered teeth he promises to return.

And he does. Twenty-two short minutes later he walks through the open door and closes it behind him. He shuffles straight to the edge of the cockeyed bed and throws a c-note (a hundred dollar bill) on the pillow. An 8-ball of cocaine bounces next to it. My body trembles in exhilaration. Thrilled. Face aglow as if I've seen the Holy Child.

This response brings delight to his ashy cheeks. He passes me the torn-off corner of his Winston pack. "Put dat up fa saf' keepin'. It my numba." I spring from the bed, throw both arms around his neck and kiss his dusty forehead. His eyes blush, cause his face won't show red. Then he turns. Out the door he wanders void of his usual focus.

I snort line after line. Light a new cigarette long before the former one's gone. I give the maid money to bring me a fresh pack of smokes each day. That way I'm not without. Forgot what hungry feels like, but got plenty of change for the soda machine. Money stretches further without the expense of food.

Snorting powder makes you hot. An hour ago I turned on the heater. Getting chilly.

Cocaine makes me nervous—especially if it's been awhile. I feel like people can tell I'm high. The quiet rustic atmosphere transforms shaky into damn near alarmed. It's been over six hours. I keep trying to talk myself into going outside.

I can handle it now. I think.

Constantly reassuring myself, I unlatch the door. Down the walkway I trot looking only in front of me. With as little conversation as possible I pay the phone deposit. I stop at the soda machine on the way back. Feels like everyone's watching.

I call the number for Jo-Jo. No answer. I don't mind, too high to talk to him right now anyway. Been here more than a week and haven't heard a word from him. Don't believe it. Maybe he's scared because it's South Carolina and I'm white. I don't know? Scared? Not Joseph Jackson.

Night settles in and the shimmer of lightning-bugs flash beyond the dim porch light. I'm cold. Must be a fever. Am I sick?

Before long, chills quake my innards. The flu. Great! Just what I need. Covered from my heels to my chin with the plaid nylon bedspread, awareness starts to fade. Then, without warning, soda pop and stomach acid shoot from my gut to the foot of the bed. High will keep you from a lot of things but throwing up ain't one of them.

Draped over the toilet for hours I feel like I'm dying. I'd rather be dead. My ears pound in hot delirium. My swallow is painful. Constricted. Lonely rejection and lack of concern disrupt what's left of consciousness. I want my Mommy.

Cool rags, a warm bath, prayer. Nothing helps. I crawl from the bathroom floor to the phone and ring Hide's number. No answer. I leave a weepy message.

A knock wakes me. I survey my surroundings. I'm half naked with thin, caramel colored, vomit everywhere. Oh yeah, I remember, I'm in South Carolina on the bathroom floor. Hours have passed, I can tell by the light. My brain feels like it's on fire. Can't lift my head from the cold tile. I try to yell. A scarce whimper is all that escapes me.

Footsteps. Someone's inside. Hope it's Jo-Jo.

Hide calls out. "Texy, Texy? Where ya at, Texy?" I strain to kick the wall. Peeking around the edge of the door, he discovers me. "You a'ight Texy?"

Situations have a tendency to tattle on you. Hide's a fine hillbilly of a black man, with a huge heart—that's what this one tells. He helps me up and straightens me out. Keeps his eyes tilted downward, to avoid staring at my undressed parts. Once covered in the nearest clothes, he loads me into his truck. A few blocks up the hill we take a right and pull alongside an old two-story brick building.

"Don' fret nun, Texy. It be on the firs flo'." He announces and hurries around to the passenger's side. Kicking the resistant truck door open wide, he picks me up, and carries me into the Mountainside Clinic.

Next thing I remember I'm home. Naples. My brain's empty when I consider how I got there. Not sure. But I'm at my parent's. All I *can* guarantee you is I never did see Jo-Jo.

★ ★ ★

Mom's a mess. Devastated by the reality of who her daughter's become. I don't care. She can't fix me. Even if she can, I won't let that happen. Ask me and all her fixing's what got me here in the first place. She never cares when it matters to me and cares way too much if it matters to her. She's got five million answers. None of which work or make a bit of sense for that matter. She doesn't get me. Never will.

Friends and family tell me I need help. They swear I can't do it on my own. I'm not dumb or anything, just always been able to do whatever I put my head to. I don't need help. I don't. But they won't let up.

Disgusted.

12

WITH THE SPOON

Hey diddle diddle,
The cat and the fiddle,
The cow jumped over the moon.
The little dog laughed,
To see such sight,
And the dish ran away with the spoon.

The old Florida home is wrapped with a large wooden porch. It's at the end of a dirt road that brings to mind a slave farm or the Amityville Horror. Not exactly a place you want to be left. Teen Challenge. A Pentecostal organization. Twenty girls live here. Coming from an uptight, proper Southern Baptist background convinces me these people are whacked. And the rules. My god are there rules. I'm not in the habit of following reasonable rules and these are ridiculous. Church equals rules. That's the way that goes and I'm disgusted with both.

My brother and his girl are acting as excited as possible when we pull up to the huge, rundown house. No one can believe I agreed to this—including me.

This is crazy, man. I can't do it. What will these people expect of me. Why did I agree to this crap? These are my softer thoughts. Be sure of this: I don't wanna be here. Buddy opens the door of their brown Oldsmobile 88, while Dorothy turns around and tries to encourage.

"You'll be fine, Texas. You can do this."

I feel aggravated at myself. Whatever insane notion urged me in this direction is a million miles removed in this moment.

"You're kidding, right? You people plan on leaving me here? This is help?" But deep inside something refuses to disappoint. Life's getting profane. Don't really have anywhere to go—nowhere worth being. Guess I'll give this a shot.

"Okay. I'll stay," I say. As soon as the words launch from my lips, Buddy hightails it to the trunk and begins unloading my things.

Who knows? Could work? Maybe I'll have a sense of fulfillment when it's over. Deep in my soul I believe there's a better way.

I strut up the stairs to the house with my same old know-it-all attitude. The one all teenagers have. The ladies stare, shrug their shoulders, or roll their eyes. Some look on with excitement, relieved to have a new victim. Others wear that "poor-child" expression. A few girls stand in the back with bright-eyed smiles, and a recognizable glow of contentment. Those faces are what keep me from a sharp u-turn.

With a final farewell to Buddy and Dorothy, I follow the director to the back office. I sit in the wooden chair across from his huge desk. Uncomfortable. The back wall is lined with books. Reminds me of the principal's office at the Christian school; not a happy memory. Titles like Faith Can and Grace Will are stamped on the multicolored spines. Tall, long, fat, wide, stout, thin. You'd think they'd have the answer after all this research. Members of the world-wide church organization have been investigating and examining this stuff for years. None of it calculates well. Not with me.

★ ★ ★

Childlike faith holds tight. Or could it just be the law of cause and effect. This cause is bound to bring better effect than the other one. I'm certain God's real and that He can do anything, but He's supposed to be motivated by love. The people who claim to follow Him are impatient and critical. None of them are too thrilled by me. Doesn't look like love.

Please Lord, show me how life's supposed to work. I'm here. So do something, will you?

Pastor Randy Ross is a cute, excitable, fireball of a man. Never seen a preacher hop across the stage on one foot—Bible flapping in hand. Not a Baptist. At church, the congregation sits on the edge of their seats in anxious anticipation of a touch from the Holy Spirit. People speak gibberish and writhe around on the floor. Strange stuff. I roll my eyes at first but before long I find myself questioning. Is this God? Is it possible? Never have been able to explain His power, have we?

It goes against what's familiar, but something's happening in me. Excited about church for the first time in forever. I feel God's presence like never before. Even lost my footing last Wednesday night when they prayed over me. Could this be authentic?

At night the girls make fun. Giggles echo down the hall as they imitate Mrs. Fisher. "Glory, glory, glory. Send power, Father. Your power." I don't laugh. It isn't funny. A bit dramatic—no doubt—but God's power is real. If you believe the Bible, crazier things than this have happened. And His word says His character doesn't change. Figure it out.

Interested. Moved even. Can't dismiss the possibility. I won't. I tell my parents when they visit. "This is real, you guys. Really real. I know it is."

In less than a week I have a pal. Teresa Simon. I'm 18, she's 26. She's from New Orleans. Her hubby, Jax, and her are long-time junkies. Heroin. He's a Cajun. Folks from those parts are proud people with thick culture. She's tired of that old life, but can't bear to consider life without him.

She always talks of home. Their traditions gain my interest. Stories of fat Mrs. Dupree falling into the Bayou while fetching a crawfish trap. Andre Alexander's famous jambalaya. And don't forget Mardi Gras—the party of a lifetime. The way they talk, dress, and eat. A whole different world. Like red beans and rice, they stick together. Looking back I see this is what draws me most. Community.

Resa's electric personality and dazzling enthusiasm fascinate me. Hope I'm this fun at her age. We make up songs and dances. We play pranks on each other and everyone else. She makes life here great fun.

Submission. A hard concept. Can't recall the incident, but in a moment of angry rebellion we toss our bags over our shoulders and down the dirt road we walk. Not one dollar in palm. They can't keep us here but they certainly won't finance our departure.

My bag's heavy. A week ago, a lady from our home church, sent me fifteen brand-new beautiful outfits. She owns an expensive boutique on the fine side of Naples. "Please take these to Texas, Cathee. I hope it will encourage her new direction."

I'm grateful. Been serious about giving this a go but once my switch is tripped—I'm off. Best I can tell, rebellion's mucked up my life most. It's push is enough to cause Smokey the Bear to start lighting forest-fires.

Some dude at the bus station buys us tickets. "Can't leave you pretty ladies out here with no way home. My luck, I'll read about you in the paper tomorrow. Can't live with that."

New Orleans, better watch out.

★ ★ ★

Hollywood provides my only info on drug injection. Even they don't show it much. Imagination's deceptive. My first shot of heroin isn't fun. It's what they call a rinse. Leftovers from what the person before shot. Truth to tell, there's nothing in the spoon. My intense headache proves that.

Maybe it's best. Don't shoot up again for years. Didn't catch a buzz but what I do catch is Hepatitis C. First shot. Don't find out till rehab but that's what happened.

Resa's way different. Rude and hostile. Her eyes are often closed or closing. Nodding. It happens when you do downers. I'm bored. Don't like this drug or the needle. I need some cocaine.

Her husband Jax is smart and funny. He thinks the world of me. He calls me New-Money.

"Down hea in Cajun Co'ntry dey's nutin' bettea dan nu' mon-e. Ya hea me, gurl."

He's a good-looking man, oozing with matter-of-fact conviction, and stunning charm. The more distant I am from Theresa, the closer we get. They argue whenever she doesn't have dope.

The neighbor, Ken, is a kind, hard-working man with a beautiful home. He's nuts for me. No thanks. Still he gives me his door key. Hoping, I'm sure.

"What's a fine woman like you doing with these trashy people? They're a disaster, Texas. You don't belong with the likes of them."

These two stay too high to talk and too mad to smile. I mostly hang with Ken—when he's home.

One morning while Resa's gone to pickup her daily dose of methadone from the clinic, and Ken is at work, Jax comes in with five huge pieces of freebase. Never say never. His witty persuasion of my need to show gratitude lands us in bed. The choice isn't hard. Paid for my emotional needs this way for years. Just never been encouraged by drugs and never with a friend's man. Unless you count Billy, and I don't.

Who forgot to lock the door?

Teresa opens it and finds us half-naked. She goes nuts like I've never seen. Enraged. She charges at me, eyes ablaze with vengeance. Jax drags her home in his boxers and I spend the night at Ken's.

Been staying here a lot anyway. It's safe. He doesn't use drugs and respects women. When morning comes, Ken calls me to the front porch. Doesn't know about yesterday. He was at work.

"Come out here, Texas. What did I tell you about those two." I peek from the door to find my clothes all over the porch. Ripped and dirty. The uncommon feeling of fear kidnaps me. Can't stay here anymore.

I phone home. Dad answers. I tell him what happened, leaving out my fault in the matter. Without a second thought he says, "The only thing I'll do for you, Texas, is pick you up at the Sarasota airport and drive you to the Life Program. I won't even pay for your plane ticket."

My head swirls. My heart stirs. What should I do?

Mixed.

13

BLIND MICE

Three blind mice. Three blind mice.
See how they run. See how they run.
They all ran after the farmer's wife,
Who cut off their tails with a carving knife,
Did you ever see such a sight in your life,
As three blind mice?

Arms flap with barbaric vigor. They call it "motivating." You have to do it in group to be called on. It looks like a seizure of sorts. What on earth have I gotten myself into? Twelve months of in-patient and an additional six out. This is no do-gooder, churchy program. It's real rehab.

My younger brother, Curtis, is here. One beer too many guaranteed his immediate incarceration. Mom and Dad wouldn't dare risk another negative outcome. He's doing great. On third phase. There are six phases before you seven-step (graduate). Sammy, the girl from Naples, the one who drove me to first meet Jo-Jo. She's completed the program and is on staff here. Can you believe that?

I'm a dreaded Newcomer. I must be belt-looped wherever I go. This is when your assigned Oldcomer holds you by the back waist band of your pants. You can't do or go anywhere without them. Intense program, no doubt.

Parents come to Friday night open meetings. Across this forum they announce to the room things you've done and how it made them feel. You aren't allowed to respond. Shameful. The experience awakens emotions we've all kept silent. For the group it forms an honest unity. It's designed to break kinship with what was.

Won't take you through the entire eighteen months but my brother and I both seven-step. Things that would never have been addressed or resolved in our family history were dealt with here. Mixed emotions find their proper places. No regrets.

On Sixth Phase—the outpatient part—I am able to get a job. After a few other tries I finally land my dream job. A beauty consultant for Lancome Cosmetics. I'm good at beauty stuff. How I look is where I find value. Helping others with this is great fun.

The job's a glammed-up role at a high-end department store in the mall. Coastland Mall. Only ten blocks from the projects. Doesn't bother me. I'm wholly committed to this new way of life. I miss the old but the new has much more to offer. That's clear now.

Naples isn't big. Many people I know come traipsing past my counter but I feel, deal, and heal. I talk about it in group and work through my steps. One day, a dear friend of mine from high school stops by the counter. I'm so excited to see her. She was my most fun friend.

Robin Dawson. A tall and rowdy rocker. Long blonde, perfectly feathered hair, and clear blue eyes. Beautiful. She uses, but we never did drugs together. Won't affect me. I can go back to who I was when we hung out. The program promises different but I swear I'm the exception.

We start going to Fort Myers on the weekends. Buddy and Dorothy live there and do the weekend club scene. We tag along. With only a finger's grip on sobriety, I contend I never was a drinker so a few drinks won't hurt. I need to make up for time missed in my pursuit of the illegal. When they tell you "addiction is cunning and baffling," they're not kidding.

A few weeks later, guess who shows up at the makeup counter. Billy King, that's who.

"I heard you were here and looked like a million bucks. I had ta com' see for myself. And they wadn't lyin'. No sir."

Every inch of my mind and body are totally taken with sheer delight. "Billy, Billy, I'm so glad to see you. Billy Barbie. The black Barbie." Eyes flare with passion, we laugh and remember various nicknames and inside jokes. "There's so many things to tell. How are you? I miss you. I'll always love you. No one can keep me from loving you. You know this, right?"

"Cum be my baby, Tex. I'll giv' it all up for you."

Past wrongs are absorbed by a sponge of thirsty hope for unrealized dreams. Shocked by my reaction, I wonder, is William King the love of my life? Has he always been? He's a great guy. We match. Got the same sense of humor even. He's well-dressed, well-educated, and fun-loving. I mean, if you're going to be with an ex dealer this is the kind it should be. A guy who's smart enough to want different.

Eighteen long months I spent weeding the old from the new. I raked, pruned, nurtured, and fertilized. But in an instant I'm re-infested with the same foolish lies. One unguarded encounter with the past allows destructive concepts to march straight in. Ambushed. It's not that all these things aren't true of Billy—they are. Only once you step out of bounds, the shot's no good, and we have crossed more than one foul line.

★ ★ ★

Value and prestige. Gusto and enthusiasm. My brain's all over the place. Former seductions batter my new psyche. Like a stream that falls from a twenty foot cliff, I'm drenched in a powerful rush of tumbling emptiness whose only fill was found in him. Maybe. Not sure how authentic these feelings are but I have a deep ache for this relationship.

"How's Alexandra? Are you guys still a couple?" I ask. "On-again, off-again. Neva did love her, not like I do you. Forever waitin' on the great Texas," he says with an injured smile. "So… What you gon' do?"

The rebel screams Yes. The good girl shouts No. This will never be okay. My family will be crushed. Not only that, I know what the program teaches about old places and people. I don't want that life. Do I?

I try to explain but Billy's deaf to me. His life's been crammed with defeat and now I'm an added disappointment. He can't figure how someone can be so sure of passion, yet so leery of love. No blame here. I don't get it myself. Alarmed.

"Come on Tee. You serious? You ain't willing ta give this a shot? Why not? You know how I feel 'bout you."

He's right, I do know but I also know how he treats his women. He gets angry and violent. He's never been faithful to one—not that I know of.

Caution won't let up and I say, "I can't, Billy. I can't." Without another word he storms for the exit.

A cruel stare of self-hatred peers back from the mirror in the bathroom. Tears without relent stream down spoiling my flawless make-up. Torn between separate realities I'm unsure what matters. You promised yourself you'd never walk on the heart of true love. What if this is it?

My family doesn't get me. They only like me when I'm doing what they want. Billy came here, though I was lost to him. He dumped his guts before me at great risk and I rejected him. How? Why? I'm so confused.

I wipe the black streaks from my cheeks, freshen up my face, and return to work. I make it to closing but cry the whole way home. I awake the next morning to fat eyes and a sore heart. I don't bother to tell anyone what happened. Who can possibly understand a matter that can't be explained?

Two days later I answer the house phone to a desperate voice. It's Robin's mom. Cries of hysteria make her words sound foreign. "Robin's in the hospital, Texas. She was in a car accident yesterday afternoon. She's in a coma. They don't expect her to live."

I collapse to the floor in disbelief. After I gain an inkling of composure I rush to the Fort Myers Trauma Center. The same one I end up in later. I push open the room door to my friend with a face that's almost unrecognizable.

"If you knew what you looked like, you'd get up and get dressed." I say with a halfhearted giggle. "Robin, Robin, I'm so sorry. I need to talk to you. Can you hear me? I've never told you about, Jesus. That's why I'm here. If you don't make it out of this, I couldn't stand myself if I'd never told you who He is."

I go through the awful experience of explaining God's love to my unconscious girlfriend. Heartbreaking. Then I leave the hospital with as much comfort as can be found in the situation. Robin dies later that night.

The program would forbid our weekend adventures so they too have remained hushed. I thought I was strong and mature, but I can't handle this. Not coupled with last week's visit from The King.

Crippled by the fear of revealing these emotions, I'm left to bear the weight of both losses alone. This blend of circumstance churns itself into a potion as deadly as hemlock. Tortured in the darkness by swirling sorrow, yesterday's solutions resurface.

Why should I opt to feel, when I can opt out? Numb. That's what I need. If I'm gonna get numb I want to be where I can stay that way. The projects.

Billy allows me to move in. Alexandra's back. What did I expect after the mall scene? He hates alone and I get that. Still, I'm mad. Wounded and irritated by our encounter, Billy keeps busy trying to make obvious to me the cost of rejecting him.

He waits up till I come home to give Alexandra elaborate gifts. They hit the freshest clubs and hottest concerts. Worst thing? He only gives me powder when he feels like it. It's pretty ugly. If I had wanted to be forced to learn lessons, I'd have stayed where I was.

This life's insane. You do things without understandable cause, convinced it's what's best. You're selfish and senseless. How can I blame him? I can't and I don't.

The problem's with me. The past. Can't let go. Silly subjects come up and fill me with a abnormal and unfamiliar fury. Being here grows skin on naked bones I swore were dead and buried. The dreamy bells of expectation for rekindled love don't ring true.

Lost.

14

THE MONKEY CHASED

All around the mulberry bush,
The monkey chased the weasel.
The monkey thought 'twas all in good fun,
Pop! goes the weasel.

There's a new crew in town, and with them comes what people refer to as fish scale or bubblegum. Flakey cocaine with an opalescent finish. The drain it gives in the back of your throat is smooth and clean. Within minutes of doing a line, you'll think your neck has vanished. Good stuff.

I like one of them. His name is Rich. They call him Richie Rich. He has brown-sugar colored skin and charm that's every bit as sweet. They're from the south side of Tampa and they bring the charisma Naples lacks. Lost contact with Jo-Jo and they're the next best thing. Gotta get in good with these guys.

After only a few weeks, Rich is mine. We've been together a month and I'm glad to have him around. It boosts my significance. Until I find out he's sleeping with two other women and that's just in Naples. He goes to Tampa at least twice a week. The most important thing about being my boyfriend is that you're totally captivated by me. Only me. A huge fight under the tree ends in breakup. He returns with a gun and forces me into my car.

"We goin' ta Tampa. You and me."

Only a few blocks till the air in the car is packed with various explanations and professions of his love. "Babe, come on. She threw herself at me. I'm only a man. You my heart. Da only one for me. Won't happen again."

Finished. Nothing to argue about. We been fighting for over a week and now I have facts. That's all I need. I'll drive him to Tampa but this is done.

We cruise up I-75 to the Bay. At his mother's house, I run inside to use the bathroom. When I return he's disappeared, with my car. After three hours and no word from him, I'm pissed. But I might as well be a paraplegic with no wheelchair. Parked. My pager's in the car with all my numbers and I only know a few folks here.

Joyce is a baser (smokes freebase). Rarely does she show up here but today his reckless sister happens through. "What up, girl? Where ya been?" she questions.

A frantic outrage throws me into chatter. "Your dumb-ass brother left me here. You seen him? He can't make me stay with him. If he keeps this up I'll call the police. I will. I don't care. Is he nuts? He's got my car."

She shrugs her shoulders without concern. The only reason she's happy to see me is in hopes of a free high but I'm on E. Nothing but my purse, less than 20 bucks, and my girly appeal—of course.

"What ya gon' do na, gurl?" Joyce questions.

"No clue. Any good ideas?" I respond with a sunshiny tone of expectancy.

"Come-on, gurl. Jus com wit me. We'll get inta somthin'."

Down the dingy uneven sidewalk we go, headed who knows where. Houses on the street are small and uniform. All lined up like colorful preschool blocks. Barely a space between them. The further we go the more people we see. Guys sport jeweled teeth and Kango hats. Girls wear anything bright and tight. Music vibrates blocks in advance, from cars with loud paint jobs. You never see this in Naples.

Girls that aren't female, walk dogs that aren't tame. Shoes that match purses, hats, or hair color. The entertainment and bustle puts you in mind of a circus. A partyer's amusement park. Not only that, everyone's got something to say when I strut past.

"Joyce, who ya got dere?"

"Cum hear, Blondie. I got somethin' for ya."

"Neva seen a white gurl with dat much ass."

"Where y'all headed? Can I go?"

Joyce doesn't look to the right or left. Doesn't speak to anyone—including me. Just one foot in front of the other. Focused.

"Where we goin'?" I ask.

"Shut up," she says and grabs my arm. "Jus keep walkin'." I roll my eyes but wouldn't think of turning back. No clue where we're headed but I'm certain what'll be there. Freebase. I promised myself never again. Again. But today it's game on.

We turn a corner and the rude sun is blocked by a dilapidated apartment building. A touch further and we duck through some brush into an abandoned cul-de-sac. Before us stands a little house. A shack. Nothing green lives within a hundred feet of the place. The fence around it is collapsed in spots, as if an elephant sat on it. The windows have boards that are spray-painted black. Not a real inviting joint.

I follow her straight to the door. A guy in sunglasses, and more gold than Rumpelstiltskin, nods at Joyce and opens the door.

★ ★ ★

Inside it's drab yet infested with people. Stand in here too long and you'll pull a plus sign on a drug screen. Sure thing. My eyes burn and leak tears.

"I need the restroom," I say.

"It over der." Joyce nods. "Go'on, gurl, I'll be rite here."

There's water and electricity—even toilet paper. I use the bathroom, check my makeup, and return. No Joyce. An older lady stands by the front door with an intense look. Stunned. Listening way too hard. Several people feel around on the floor as if in search of a lost contact. A tall, scarecrow of a man stands in a corner talking to himself and swatting nonexistent flies. The place is crowded but feels empty at the same time.

To the left there's a blue velvet, wingback chair. Next to it there's a large boombox. It plays old-school slow jams. Love this music. The rest of the room is loaded with crippled sofas, folding chairs, and homemade benches. Cans, bottles, and ash trays are everywhere. The kitchen's roped off. Before the cord there's a beat-up, overflowing trash can. The kind that usually camps alongside the garage.

The A/C blows cold but people are sweaty. Every race imaginable is here. Thin and dirty. Dressed and showy. No one cares about the other but one thing's sure, there's no place they'd rather be.

The man on the blue throne waves me over. "What ya doin hea', gurl? Pleny whiteys com' thru, but none lookin' lik' you. Damnit, you fine."

"Came to party like everybody else," I say.

"Dat's gud news. Gud for me anyway." His eyes twinkle as he looks me up and down. He stands and heads towards a door that's bolted tighter than Donald Trump's vault. Pulling keys from his pants, he tilts his head in the direction of the door. "Wanna party wit me?"

"Don't know you and I ain't from here. If you think I'm going in some locked room with you, you're outta your pea-picking mind."

"Car'ful, whitey, I don' pick shit. Wrong nigga." He's pissed. I don't care. "Neva back down," that's what Jo-Jo says.

"Point is, I got plenty of sense. You tried me with that bullshit." I raise both hands with a smart aleck expression to indicate he left me no choice.

He eases back into his chair where a line of people wait. He unzips the pouch that hangs from his neck and begins to fill orders. Tens and twenties, gold watches and chains. Stereos—even a roll of quarters. All in exchange for the magic rock.

"Jus so it all add up. Dat's what matta," he says.

Still no Joyce. I pull up a chair and sit down. Disappointed.

"I like you, gurl. Day call me Stick. Pull out ya pipe and let me help ya get started. Who know wat'll cum if I get ya on it." He smirks and winks.

"Don't have one," I shrug.

Drawing a five from his pocket, he calls over a dwarfed Spanish man. The tiny dude heads straight for the door without a word of instruction. Back in a wink. Within two minutes his strangely black palms have constructed a pipe. He hands it to Stick and walks away.

"Cuba. Show her how ta work dis thang. She green."

He's quick to instruct me through the procedure. "Got it?" he asks.

"I got it." For the next few hours Stick throws me a piece every time I'm out. Wonder what he's expecting.

We laugh and joke. Make fun of people. He pets my hair on occasion and slaps my ass when I stand. No problem. Joyce shows up from nowhere to help me—smoke that is. I don't mind. It's free and I'd be at her mom's freaking out if it wasn't for her.

"I'm gone in 10. You comin' wit me," Stick asks? "I'll show ya what da Bay Area 'bout."

Why not? Nothing better to do. "Okay, I'll come."

Joyce stands in protest. Too high to speak full voice, she hisses, "Not alone, she ain't. Not long as I got breath."

Stick gets mad. Real mad. He cusses and shouts harsh names and charges straight for her. Fierce. Then comes the sound, so loud my ears ring. A gun shot. No idea which direction it came from. The room is filled with pandemonium. Consumed by a smell similar to burnt plastic.

A harsh-faced, tiny woman slams a chair across the boarded window. It bursts open. Joyce yanks at me. The two of us scramble into the daylight. Down the street we sprint in the direction we came from. We take a corner that lands us on the main drag. Pointing ahead she says, "Six blocks down, take a lef', firs' house on da rite. I'm goin' back. Somebody mighta lef' somethin'."

Been in Tampa for three days. No word from Rich. I scrounge through my wallet and happen across the number.

The gambling house in Naples. I can picture the men there hunched in the corner, neat ends of money sticking from one hand while dice click about in the other. Bet they miss me. I bring luck. That's what they tell me.

Under the tree. It's the place to be if you're across the tracks in River Park. A little encouraged fantasy should get me a ride home. I dial the phone.

Someone picks up. First ring. It's Bubba. His brother runs the spot. Bubba's always flirting and coming on to me. He thinks I'm the prettiest girl alive. Ideal. I'm sure he'll come.

Bubba doesn't have a car but within hours he's on his way. Thank god. I'm out of here. He catches a ride with Boogie. Boogie sells powder so there's plenty of that for the ride home.

My hero. We get a room and sometime during the next 24 hours I sleep with Bubba. Not because I have to. He's different from other men. The usual pressure of expectancy is missing. He's just happy to be with me. Could this be true love?

Caught.

15

QUITE CONTRARY

Mary, Mary, quite contrary,
How does your garden grow?
With silver bells, and cockle shells,
And pretty maids all in a row.

We're inseparable. Bubba's a good man, not a run-around-the-street kinda guy. Comes from a big family. He lives with his brother and cares for his three month old little girl, Brittany. Not sure what happened but her mom moved to Titusville. Don't normally like children but I really like Britt-Britt. I move in with a friend across from them.

Things are going great until *she* shows up. The baby's momma. Only been back a few days but already she's cussing, yelling, and throwing things. Never ran into a problem like this in the projects. Don't like being caught in the middle. Bubba acts like he can't stand her. Says he's done everything possible to make her realize. I'm not scared. Just don't care for the drama.

One night at a huge block party, I walk inside to get a drink. Everybody's here. When I look down the hall I see Bubba standing over his ex. Arm on her shoulder. I've been blaming her and it's him. He's playing us both. I push my way to where he is, and when he turns I pound on his chest. "How dare you. I hate you. It's over." (I'll spare you the exact quote.)

I rush from the house in a rage. On the inside my heart thumps with pain I'm too proud to acknowledge. The heat of anger won't cool. Demented by unexpected rejection.

Then I hear a motorcycle. Maybe that's Fish. Must be. No one else around here rides a motorcycle. Fish is a cute but strange guy. He loves white girls.

My eyes surge with fury, as if my thoughts are looking for escape. People are laughing and talking trash. The place thrives on this kind of upheaval. Fish waits for the perfect moment then rolls up.

"Jump on. What you needin' is a gud ride. Don't worry wit dis junk. Cum wit me. I'll make ya forget all 'bout dis bullshit."

"Where we goin'?" I say.

"You care?"

"No. Let's do it." I hop on the back and we ride. The rush of wind in my ears distracts but not near as much as the duplex we pull up to.

"This you?" I question.

"Sur-nuf." His warm smile shines through the mask on the helmet. He helps me from the bike. Shouldn't be surprised at the condition of his place. Don't really know this dude. Scuzzy. A godforsaken hole. What on earth happened to the glamorous life?

The mud-smudged door swings open and an old woman mumbles an indecipherable sentence. I follow his lead past her into a trashy living space. A small shriveled man sits on a rusty folding chair. He stares at a fuzz-filled TV screen. Never looks our way but shouts, "Ay."

Fish grabs my arm to keep me headed in the right direction. He walks to a room, turns the knob, and pulls me in.

Locks the door behind us. A chick so thin you could use her for a science project stares intently from a mattress on the floor. No doubt it came from the caved in sofa out front.

"I'm his woman. Carol. Met you once before. Texas, right?" her golf-ball eyes nervously fixed on the pipe in her hands. Hooked.

Freebase. There's freebase. Yes!

Judgment and reservation take off. I drop to the space on the floor beside her. Like a humbled slave in need of the master's assistance I tilt my head towards Fish. "Can I be next?"

Fish laughs. His joy comes from a deep place of freedom. "Think I gotcha hea and ain't gone look-out? You can get whatever ya wantin', Ms. Texas." Then he pulls out a fresh pipe and hands me five rocks.

The thing that makes this drug so appealing is the escape. The rush is awesome. Although it only lasts for a few minutes, in those moments I'm on top of the world. All the plagues, as well as the 10 Commandments, are gone. Nothing counts.

Fish robbed a bank eighteen years back. He's only been out of prison for some months. That's a long time to be locked up. No wonder he's cheerful. The good news? He hid the loot before they were able to find him. He sells dope but won't even touch a beer. He also has a job washing work trucks at night. All this is info to me. These bright insights instantaneously transform this trench into my new residence.

His girl Carol's the kinda girl who looks used up. In these days those are the only white girls that date black guys. I can tell Fish wants me and I work that angle well. Staying high here is as relaxed as a fat girl's favorite bra. Easy.

Thirteen days. No sleep, no food. Pepsi, Newports, and dope are all I consume. Even if I were hungry I wouldn't eat here. It smells like dead cat when his parents cook. Yes, those old people in the living room are his parents. You name it, they eat it. Anything you can tear from a pig. And who knows where the animal comes from—not a grocery store. Intestines, snouts, or ears. Feet with the hooves in place. I swear they'd eat a human if they had hot sauce. Primitive.

They speak in ebonics that even a black man can't understand. A lousy environment. But none of that matters. Fish keeps the drugs flowing. That's enough. Amazing what you'll put up with when you're waiting on the next hit.

Fish is ignorant but has street smarts. He keeps all the money, guns, and drugs away from the house. That way no one will jack him, the police can't bust him, and we won't sneak into his stash while he sleeps. Sad but always a possibility when freebase is involved.

Carol and I are smoked out. Waiting, waiting. Hate this part. The tick of the clock and my clammy armpits push me to the bathroom. Not like anyone's fighting for this post. The tub is coated gray with scum and mold. No bleach or I'd clean. I wear my socks in.

I use a bar of soap, washrag, and towel I stole from the store. Gotten pretty good at shoplifting over the years. Why pay? I can converse with the clerk and steal at the same time. An achievement that holds its own rush. I lather my face and work my way down. My hand glides over my chest. Ouch! Did I bump into something? I search for a bruise but there's not one. Trying to recall possibilities I wash the other side—the pain is equal. Unusual.

Shock paralyzes me when I go to wash between my legs. My god, how long since I've had a period? Alarm yanks me from the shower, still sudsy. What if? What will I do? My only relief comes in knowing the baby is Bubba's.

Bubba! I have to tell him. He's been looking everywhere for me. Last week he saw me on the road and chased me all the way to 7-11. While I was getting gas, he got down on one knee and begged me to come with him. I was headed to cop dope so his speech was irrelevant—sounded like Charlie Brown's teacher. At least five miles from the projects. What do I do? He has to know.

When all else fails, start walking. A cute girl never walks more than two blocks. I catch a ride in minutes. When I arrive the lights are off. I knock on the window where he sleeps. My fearful expression hurries him to the front door. Before I can oppose, he's pulled me inside.

"What's wrong, baby? Come here. Are you okay?"

I tell him what's going on. His eyes begin to water. He hugs and kisses me, all over my face and stomach. "This is the best news ever. Don't you worry none. Daddy will take care of you both."

He begins to spout out all kinds of plans. Not what I expected but it sure feels good. The insistent call of cocaine resounds in my ear. Gotta go. Fish is definitely back by now.

"I'll be back first thing in the morning, Bubba."

"You crazy? Now that you back, you ain't leavin'. Besides you havin' my baby." Realizing the jones for dope will get bad and I may take off when he sleeps, he says, "Stay right here, Texas. I'll be back."

The wait seems to cause the floor in the apartment to rise. Just when I'm sure I'll be flattened to the ceiling, the door squeaks open. Bubba went to the tree and credited me some base.

"I hate this shit but I'd rather you be here." That's what he says when he throws the rocks on the table. My hands rush to the tabletop collecting the pieces. I can feel my eyes radiate as I pull the pipe from my shoe.

Morning comes. I'm still here. Planned Pregnancy is a short walk down the street. We're the first ones there. Nine o'clock on the dot. A storm of fear and enthusiasm churn within me. After the usual information form is completed, I slip into the sterile bathroom and fill the cup with golden evidence.

It's official. Gonna have a baby. How will I make this work? Can't do both. Drugs or motherhood?

Conflicted.

16

QUEEN OF HEARTS

*The Queen of Hearts
She made some tarts,
All on a summer's day;
The Knave of Hearts
He stole those tarts,
And took them clean away.*

"New Hope Ministries." The receptionist answers with a cheer that irritates me.

"May I speak to Cathee Poulsen?" Mom's only worked here a few weeks.

"One moment please." Then comes the music.

What on earth will I say? I've only known fifteen minutes myself. Maybe I'll wait till…

I turn to hang up but the sound brings memories that freeze me.

"This is Cathee," comes her voice. The same one that read me nursery rhymes. Sang in the car on long road trips, recited Bible verses, or gave perfect cookie-baking instruction. My mom. I draw in air, hoping the right words will form.

"Hey, Mom. It's me."

"Texas. So glad you called. You would have loved the sermon last night. I wish…"

"I'm pregnant, Mom." Her previous kite of life-saving information plummets to the earth, caught in the crosswind of surprise. Heat gathers in my palm. The phone gets shaky. Fright soars through the wires straight down my eardrum and into my heart.

"Well, Texas, what are you going to do?"

"Have a baby. That's what."

What else is there to do? Abortion or adoption are not a consideration. Not conflicted about that. I mean that's what you do when you get pregnant. Have a baby. We talk a few more minutes and somehow I feel better. Not because of anything she says, just because she knows.

I call several times in the next week. When she asks, I'm honest about my inability to remain straight. Excitement or fear? Not sure which shoves harder but I don't hesitate to accept her invitation to move home.

Azlynn Blair Stready. That's her name. Born 8-5-89. Six pounds, thirteen ounces, and in perfect health. The nurse is taking her vital signs now, but she's fine. I can tell. I'm her mom, you know.

"Everything seems okay," she says handing her back to me. "The baby tested positive for cocaine, Texas. So did you. You're a danger to your child. I'm afraid we can't leave the two of you alone. HRS is sending a case-worker over to sit with you. They'll decide what happens next."

The charge nurse huffs from the room sporting a scowl of pure disgust. Her eyes are cold. Mean. They activate a powerful yet pathetic insecurity.

An ironclad defense rises from my toes to my nose. "No way," I say to Bubba. I turn to my parents. "They can't take her from me, can they? That can't happen. Not ever." I want to cry but a fierce need to protect won't let me. I have to do something. No idea what, but something.

I engulf her petite body into mine. Tears gather in my tired eyes. I study her glorious face. Features, skin, fingers with tiny nails, feet with tiny toes. She's absolutely perfect and she's mine. A gentle kiss to her forehead is not enough. I continue kissing until I've touched every piece of her small face. Cheeks, lips, chin, and nose. The smell of her skin is familiar. Significant. It grants me a desire to do more than survive.

I'm so stupid. Dumb, dumb, girl. I know I'm the one who did this but that was all before. Before I'd seen her face, touched her lips, breathed in her presence. It was only a few lines. Does that even count? Geez. Why in the world did I do it?

I'm powerless. Can't help it. Isn't that what they say?

I have to find a way to stay clean. I can do it. I must. *God, help! Please help me be a good mom. One who cares about what's going on with my daughter. Let me keep her and I'll never do cocaine again.*

The promises of God's Word rush in. Bringing light. Forgiveness, redemption, restoration—they're possible. Bold determination takes charge. It's accompanied by the longing required to fight this perilous battle and cross the minefield of addiction.

The tower of responsible life seems miles high. Where's that damn Rapunzel when you need her? I'm a mother now. Gotta be there for my girl.

"Hi Azlynn. I'm your mommy." Her eyes blink soft and wet. "Oh, her? Don't worry about her," I say motioning towards the attendant. "She can't get you. No one can. Not ever."

With an open palm I wipe through the tears that slide from my face and puddle on my collarbone.

Shame invades an untouched part of me, promising to never leave. Lack of peace disrupts my speech. "I'm so sorry, sweet girl. Mama's sorry. You're the best thing that's ever happened to me. I love you. With all that I am, I love you. It will be okay. I promise."

Where do I hide from this boiling damnation? How can I have failed her so miserably already? How will I be different? Can I be different?

Within three months I complete the state's requirements and obtain full custody of my baby. There's nothing I want more than to be an excellent mother. Her daddy loves us both with solid intensity and I love him too. He's not much of anybody but he's dedicated. No real job, no place or car—heck, not even a driver's license. But he's mad about Texas. In my head that's what matters most. Commitment.

We're working on the other stuff.

I love the Lord and He loves me. I also understand and believe the Bible is true. Naturally being with my parents I'm more involved in church. This activity ignites a fire that's been without oxygen. Reheats my desire for change. Not sure if I'll be able to walk it out but I want the life God's promised me.

We wait till Azlynn is one before we marry. Don't want to make two mistakes. My family likes Bubba. He's a hard worker with a soft heart. Besides being a bouncer at a club, he works miscellaneous jobs. He'll do anything to take care of us. I have mad respect for his love and concern for our daughter. He's the one I waited for. This will definitely last forever.

The beautiful September day arrives. I wait in the church nursery dressed in my breathtaking, champagne-colored gown. Dad steps into the room in an all black tuxedo. Sharp.

"Everyone's out there waiting and I know you're excited. I'm not saying you shouldn't do this, all I'm saying is if you're not sure, you don't have to."

"Thank you, Daddy. I'm sure. Let's do it." I smile, kiss him, and loop my arm through his.

The song begins, the people stand, and we're off. I look ahead. Down front I see my bridesmaids dressed in pale peach. My husband-to-be stands waiting, a grin stretched from one ear to the other.

Buddy works in golf course maintenance. Some fancy-pantsy golf club. A position becomes available and he gets my husband on there. We move to the next city over. Ft. Myers. Buddy and Dorothy live here too. I love my brother but our relationship is strained. He's disappointed in the way my life's turned out.

He and my mother act the same. Either of them would love to make a detailed diagram of exactly what I should do. If you ask me, most of my problems are their fault. They should have given me the time of day when it mattered.

Whatever. That's over now. I have a husband and family. My own life.

Ft. Myers is a larger town. Housing's cheaper. Especially in our neighborhood. A canal of grass separates our building from my brother's place. Bubba has his license now, but we only have one car. This setup gives him a ride to work with my brother. He leaves me the car for shopping and doctor's appointments.

Better than any of that is Buddy's girlfriend. Dorothy. She's a Puerto Rican girl with eight siblings. They were all born and raised here. She's been through a world of pain and trouble. Although we're different in our choice patterns, she gets me. She's been in our lives for five years now. Never felt closer to anyone. She's the greatest. Best thing that ole' Budrow could dream of.

Weekends are made for hanging out. Other cultures seem better at this practice than white people. Friday by 6 PM we're ready. Tables set up between the apartments. Cooler's full, grill's hot, and cards dealt. Dorothy knows everybody, so getting a sitter is easy. When money affords, we head straight for the bar. Drink City. The freshest club in town.

I'm not much of a drinker but I'll always be a pothead. No street running or drug hustling makes using cocaine as rare and expensive as a red diamond. Bubba and I run across some on occasion.

When the circling lasso does fall over our heads it yanks hard. A half gram becomes three, leaving us in the poorhouse till the next payday. How idiotic. The same thing's always true. When your eyes open the next day, an immovable mountain of regret stands laughing in your face—fingers wrapped tightly around your throat. Scandalous.

Can't complain. All in all, life's good. I think. As close as I remember since my days of creek-searching and donkey-taming. Those days are forever gone. Something below the surface has shifted never to settle into ignorant bliss again.

Azzie's a smart girl. A pro at learning. And I love teaching her. She sang Happy Birthday on her first birthday and is swimming at 18 months. What a team we make. Me and my girl.

When I was young I didn't make plans for my future. No real dreams. That's how you dodge letdown—or so I thought. I'm a make-the-most-of-it kinda girl. I knew I'd be married and have kids, but never envisioned my wedding or named my children. This life is fine by me. I'm irreplaceable to these two. That's all I ever wanted.

Love.

17

SURE TO GO

Mary had a little lamb,
His fleece was white as snow,
And everywhere that Mary went,
The lamb was sure to go.

It's never enough. No matter how much I clean, how well I cook, or how often we have sex, my husband's always unhappy. My belly's swelled with our second child. The sonogram says it's a boy. Bubba's so excited. He wants to name the poor child Grover Stready, the Third. No way! Eight months pass before I get weak.

"I know this is important to you, so we'll name him Grover but he'll have a middle name. Jordan. And that's what we'll call him. Okay?"

Jordan rolls in on the scene three weeks early. The same birthday as my grandmother and me—November 7th. Amazing. A special guy. The cutest little sucker you've ever seen. He's calm, sweet, and man is he crazy about his momma.

Even as the years pass all he wants is me. Love hardly describes my feelings for him. He's better than the first one. Well, not really. Never thought I could love anyone as much as Azzie. Now I can't imagine life without my boy. He's not like his big sister. She's a firecracker with a mind of her own. Wonder who she got that from?

Bubba's an alcoholic. It took a long time to see but it's true. He drinks every night. When he gets drunk there's no reasoning with the man. He gets angry. Hostile. I'm not real good at keeping my opinion to myself. My dad and Curtis are the only Poulsens who can do that. I must be heard. I will be understood. This mindset doesn't mix well with drunk.

Addiction cripples truth but pointing the finger would require I let go of my own crutch. Don't want to do that. No matter what craziness goes on I'm sure my husband loves me, the children, and the Lord. That's as good as it gets when you start off where we did.

Bubba's no longer at the Bonita Golf Club. We're back in Naples. He's a cook on Third Street. Nice restaurant. Learned to decorate watching Mom, so I keep a beautiful home. My kids are involved in everything and the family attends church regularly. Bubba rides in his own car and leaves the moment the service ends—but at least he goes.

Money's scarce. We have two cars, two kids, and rent is higher. Gotta do something. Don't want to get caught shoplifting so I grab some trees (pot) and get to work. Why buy when you can smoke for free?

Love my weed. Glad to be smoking again. Didn't smoke the last two months of my pregnancy with Jordan. Don't need HRS involved. I figure God won't mind. Better than the other stuff.

Life's a letdown. No one's meeting my needs. I never leave the house without both kids. It's not fair to leave them here with him watching cowboy movies—so I don't.

"Don't you want to go to Azlynn's dance recital, Bubba? Can't you walk a few blocks trick-or-treating with us?" I ask and ask but his response is always No. He's too tired from work and busy with a beer in his hand.

Can't live like this. I won't. I want it to work but I'm running out of reasons. Pain and discouragement corrode my soul. They layer my heart with scabs of heartache. We argue and fight. Go to bed angry most nights. Kids shouldn't grow up like this. I'm far from perfect but at least I try.

"We need help. This is never going to change if we don't get help. Let's go to marriage counseling," I beg. He makes occasional attempts when I threaten to leave, but there's no dedication to different.

I'm not unreasonable. I suppose no one thinks they are, in the middle of it. At this point it doesn't matter whose fault it is. Something's gotta give. The void inside's becoming too spacious to tolerate.

Been on birth control since Jordan. No period insists I take a pregnancy test. When the red plus sign shows, I make a radical decision to quit everything. Even cigarettes.

Things are rough. Two small kids, an uncooperative husband, and no weed. Yikes!

To make matters worse, my family's gone. Mom, Dad, Jed, Buddy, Dorothy and their boy, Victor, have moved to Kimberling City, Missouri. Just me and Curtis here. I babysit his son Blake, so I see him every day. Thank goodness.

Curtis is funny. Always telling jokes. The kind of person who never passes judgment. His attitude makes life better. Glad he's around. It's weird not having the rest of the family. This town leaves a rancid taste in my mouth without them. Especially sober.

Sexual sin from my father's past makes itself known in the present. Huge shock. My whole family's stunned. Not me. At this point it sorta brings everyone down to my level. Don't think my parents are running but Naples is a lot to handle. Even on a good day.

Family's important. Attempting to win mom's approval in my younger years, I took on the job of making us appear perfect. Impossible. As best I can figure drugs start as an escape from this self-declared responsibility. Prime example of how childhood ideas are twisted into the exact opposite. My behavior certainly didn't make anyone look better.

My first departure from home was a disaster. Still it brought a distorted freedom that breathed independence to my suppressed soul. I evaluate my thinking constantly but there seems to be no way to gather correct concepts in the middle of too much. Too much pain, too much shame, too much trouble, too much drug use, too much desire to please, too much damn reality—that's what. Way too much.

Hate my children being away from my family. Doesn't seem right. We make up our minds we'll move to Missouri. On the last day of June we leave our three year home and move in with family friends, awaiting our new addition. Peeking his head into the world on the 27th of July, comes Justice Kade.

Okay now he's got to be the cutest baby I have. Maybe! What can I say, it's a close competition.

Car crammed full only days later. We head for the Show-Me State in hopes of seeing a new outcome. Bubba's driving fine until we hit the mountains. If you've never driven in the mountains, trust me, it takes some getting used to. He's sick. The car's at a crawl. Don't know what I'm doing either but self-determination takes over. Baby attached to my breast and arm propped on the center console, I drive.

The mountains of Tennessee, Kentucky, and Missouri creep in and out of view as if remembered in a moment of Déjà vu. Without break for twenty-two hours we ride. Finally, into my mother's arms I collapse, practically throwing five pound Justice at her. Relief.

"We made it. We're here. Thank God!"

The only mixed couple in town. Celebrities. Bubba quit drinking about three months before we left and I've been 100% clean for eight months. Please don't get the wrong picture, I haven't exactly honored my husband throughout our marriage. I was unfaithful. More than once. Not something I'm proud of but this tale is not a pride promoter. It's about truth.

The years we spend in this hee-haw town are the happiest time in our marriage.

A friend from church makes up her mind I'll be a great addition to her Mary Kay squad. After months of asking, I give in and go to a meeting. This organization feeds my hunger for cause. Validates me. From my mountain of emptiness, I take an explosive leap and nosedive straight into the world of direct marketing.

I'm good. My director is a phenomenal woman who sees my potential and genuinely cares about me. Love the recognition. In three months I win a brand-new red Grand Am and a spot on stage at seminar with Mary Kay herself. I'm important in the real world.

The family's ecstatic. My little brother Jeddie was devastated when I left home. Now his face beams with adoration when he looks at me. Jed and his friends are always at my house. He's nuts about my children. When self-worth goes up, so does my desire to give back. I love people, it's part of who I am.

My relationship with the Lord is as close as it's ever been. I make up my mind to start a youth ministry. These kids are really sharing with me and I'm able to help. Success number two.

My sister-in-law, Dorothy, loves the name Kade. She wants me to call Justice by his middle name. I won't. She begins to call him Justicio (pronounced *hoo-stee-cio* in Spanish.) That name gets broken down to Husto. Then Hoo-Hoo. Cute. To this day we call him Hoo-Hoo.

Justice gets his first cold at eighteen months old and I'm forced to find a local doctor. When we go for the visit, the doctor insists, "As soon as Justice gets well, he must catch up on his immunizations."

Don't remember how many shot series or how often they're given, I just recall thinking it was too much. As the next year passes I begin to notice things are off with Hoo-Hoo. "Something's wrong with my baby, Dorothy. He's not right. I think he's retarded."

"Texas, don't say that."

"Something's wrong. I can tell," I repeat.

I work hard to teach him things but Justice doesn't learn at the same pace as my other children. After many questions and complaints they give him the general diagnosis of "developmentally delayed."

When you find out your child has a disability you go through a season of loss. It's worse then they think. Just one of those things a mom knows. Maybe it's because I was on birth control or all the immunizations. Then again, earlier drug use could've damaged my eggs. I'll never know. Can't help but be grateful I didn't use when I was pregnant. Couldn't live with that guilt.

Buddy and Dorothy own their house in Naples. Problems with renters force them back there. A year later my parents decide to return. We follow. Fear-induced choice is a devoted friend of disappointment. Our stable home life is under siege the moment we cross the state line.

Selling Mary Kay is hard here. It was an hour to the closest mall in Missouri. People in Naples are wealthy and have immediate access to all the latest and greatest products. Highbrows. With no ministry, no influence, and a dwindling income; my relevance begins to shrivel—like a spider doused in Raid.

From a medical standpoint I'm glad to be back. Justice is two and a half and his vocabulary is only sixteen words. He's in therapy and the doctor says he has ADHD. They put him on Adderall. Maybe this will help my sweet little boy.

The longer we're here the more I see, Bubba hasn't changed a bit. He doesn't drink anymore but he's what AA calls a dry drunk. A furious bear. Captured by the steel teeth of sober living. Didn't need his reassurance in Missouri. Had other stuff to feel good about.

Unhealed scars reappear under the microscope of disgust. This can't be happening. I've loved him so much. Tried so hard. Why? What am I supposed to do?

Abandoned at the edge of the same ole', same ole'. The projects. I ride through to say hey. Maybe old fantasies can help rebuild my collapsing castle of purpose.

"Man, gurl, did you get finer or what?"

"Neva been a white girl like ole' Texas run thru these projects."

"When you comin' ta hang wit us for a few hours, Tomcat?"

Instantly inebriated by my drug of choice. Acceptance, approval, recognition. Pathetic, I know. A clever disguise that mirrors authentic value.

We rent a beautiful home, convinced that Mary Kay sales will at least supplement Bubba's income enough to maintain. Spiritual wellness fades. This gives the former crowd an unhealthy appeal. An occasional cigarette becomes a pack a day. Smoking weed with friends grows into buying my own bag. My backwards ride on this sturdy roller coaster has me whirling in discontent. Bewitched by the tyranny of the familiar.

Bubba sees what's happening. Heartsick fury swallows him whole. His verbal slaps begin to breach the boundaries into aggression once more. It's like I reentered a nightmare after waking-up to use the bathroom. Seven years of marriage to this man and still the same old crap. I refuse to be stuck any longer. It's over.

I tell him to leave. This isn't the first time we split. But it is the last. Am I making a right turn?

Left.

18

CRADLE AND ALL

Rock-a-bye baby, on the treetop,
When the wind blows, the cradle will rock,
When the bough breaks, the cradle will fall,
And down will come baby, cradle and all.

B am, bam, bam. I can tell it's not the first round of knocks. Too insistent. I crack the blind enough to peek out. The Pontiac emblem is displayed on his hat. They're here to get the car. My sales are too low. I open the door enough to inch the keys through. "My mom said to give you these when you got here," I say. Shame's a splendid liar.

Things are going left. Fast. No car, no income, and at least $1,500 a month in bills. I'm sure Bubba won't abandon his children but he has to be able to take care of himself. Clothing and feeding three kids isn't easy. Sold drugs many times in my life, but mainly to support my habit. Never had to pay my own way. That's what a man's for.

Strike one, I pick up an ounce of weed. I pay $120 and make fifty dime bags. That brings in $500 every two weeks— minus expenses and intake. Not enough. Strike two, moves me to the quarter pound level. Before I can blink, ten dollar bags of weed become fifty dollar bags of blow (cocaine). Hey, if it don't make dollars, it don't make sense. Daily immediate access to this magic dust seduces me. That's strike three and I'm out. Out in the garage snorting lines that is. Depleted and puzzled by what feels like the only way.

The house has a pool and tile floors. Keeping up with chores is a lot of work. Before we moved to Missouri our duplex was next door to a single mother who had five children. I got real close to the two teenage girls. Shelly and Liza. They are now in the late years of high school. Got plenty of friends who smoke pot too. Decent! They'll cook, bathe children, dust furniture, even iron clothes. Anything I need they gladly do. Just to hang out. Best of all, when I credit them weed they pay. On time. Works for me.

I save every penny till I'm able to buy an older gray Mazda from a friend at church. Can't live without a ride.

Alone's not my thing. I flirt around with a few guys in search of the right man, but no one holds my interest. One afternoon I drive through the Gordon River Apartments to pick up some money I'm owed. My friend Jay talks me into smoking a gar (marijuana wrapped in cigar paper) by the park. During our smoke session, his friend pulls up in a black Ford F150.

"Jump in man, and chief wit us." Jay says.

"Hold up. Let me hit da store and get another gar. Then we'll smoke out. Bet?" he says.

"Bet," I wink.

Been in Naples sixteen years and six of them were spent in this very spot. Where's *he* been all my life? I went to school with his older sister. He remembers me but somehow I missed him. Never even heard his name before. Bizarre.

He's a cutie, but what attracts me most is his fun-loving personality. Eddie Cooper. They call him Coop. Bubba gets the kids from school today so I'm free to spend the rest of the afternoon joyfully lolly-gagging around right here.

Laughter's contagious. Just the kind of bug I'm dying to catch. Coop gets a kick out of my quirky ways. Oh how I've missed being around someone who enjoys me. His dad's a pastor and he's been raised to respect women. He also knows how to enjoy everyday life.

Can't promise to know what love looks like or if it's instantaneously possible. If so, this is it. There's only one problem. The drugs. He's done his share of hustling cocaine but has zero tolerance for people who use it. He's a weed man. Fear of rejection demands I keep my snorting undercover.

After our first sleepover we're fastened together. Glued. My clientele's small but my source is good. We combine business. In no time we are selling about five ounces a week. Early years of heavy snorting damaged my sinuses. Clogged up. Blowing bloody snot and sniffing constantly. If we get a place together he'll figure me out. No choice but to start smoking crack.

Freebase has had me on the chase a time or two but fate put it's foot down in the nick of time. New additives and fillers make crack the latest and greatest thing. Profit margins are higher and the jones is stronger. It's everywhere. I think I'm in love with him but who can tell. The drugs are making my entire life a composite of falsehoods.

Bubba works and lives at an apartment complex that's separated from our new place by only a thin wooden fence. If you get close enough you can see his back porch from between the slats—too close for comfort. He's heard what I'm up to and is treading the borders of mania. I'm defensive, not stupid. I don't want my babies around this either.

When he threatens to call the police, resentment raises its ugly head. "Oh, all of a sudden you want to be a real father. Fine, take them. They can live with you."

My kids, that were once my entire world, are becoming a bother. Years of anger clouded by billowing crack smoke, convince me I deserve a break.

Eddie wakes by 10 AM. Showers, grabs his product, and heads in-town. I sleep till at least two. When my eyes do notice light, I shoot from the bed to the back porch. I take my usual wake up in my narrow but well-equipped laundry room. It's as if the place was made for this. Next I shower. Then to the kitchen table to subtract what I smoked last night and get ready for daily sales. Good thing Coop never asks about my product or cash. By three my workers come scrabbling through. Dandy. Plenty of time to handle business and smoke myself into oblivion.

Eddie rarely comes home without calling. We stay in touch most of the day. This keeps my secret safe. One afternoon Shelly and Liza ring the doorbell. I don't answer. They make their way around back. Instead of finding me on the porch smoking a Newport, they are shocked to catch me in the laundry room—puffing on a crack rock.

They both tried soft while I was in Missouri, so I've been okay selling them powder. Nobody likes to get high alone and before long we're doing lines together. Now that they know they want to give this a go. Cocaine's bad, but this shit's a killer. Seen it disfigure many a pretty little life. Don't want to be the one to turn them on.

My morals are disheveled. I live in the clouds and look down on the earth without a true grasp on reality. Irrational. I give in to them. Such selfish irresponsibility. Still hurts my heart.

Coop rolls in between two and three most nights. Pockets packed with cash. He calls ahead so I can start dinner. I spark up the weed to silence the pulsating drum that echoes through my brain and throbs into my face. I light a scented candle. Just in case. Pork chops, green beans, mashed potatoes and gravy. And don't forget the Jiffy cornbread. His favorite.

We smoke a gar together. Then eat. Feeling mighty fine right about now. The food helps bring me down. Next we start a movie. Never make it through the flick. Too much kissing. Our friendship's deep, making passion run rampant. We enjoy each other. Thoroughly. Sex has never meant much to me. It's more like part of the deal. Can't tell if this is different, too busy anticipating the next hit.

"Go put the cookies in the oven, Boo." That's what he calls me. We like the same cookies and not too well done either. It's great. We're great.

What will I do if he ever finds out?

He falls asleep in the wee hours and I make a b-line for my smoke shop. Never have smoked cigarettes in the house. Ideal excuse if he wakes.

He won't get up though. He's tired. Been out all day and night. Besides I'm the one who serves the late nighters—there's always a few. But mainly, I get as high as Cooter Brown. Picked that phrased up in the gambling house years back.

Smoke, and smoke, and smoke. That's what I do. I get cramped and sweaty in this small space. I hate it but not enough to stop. It's the best definition for the drug. Never enough.

★ ★ ★

11 a.m., the phone rings. It's the neighbor. "The police are outside. They have dogs."

Coop just picked up the powder from its nightly hiding spot. Maybe this has something to do with Bubba. He's been pretty erratic lately. My pulse bangs in my neck when the knock comes. I turn the knob and they burst through, six deep.

Slamming me to the floor they yell, "Where's Coop?"

I'm panicked. Baffled. Before I can gather my thoughts they drag Eddie from the living room. His head hits the floor and he's cuffed. Our eyes meet and there's no halting my tears. My brain is hammered by cluttered confusion.

"Don't worry about it, Boo. Just don't say shit," he says.

Old Jo-Jo rules pour into my skull. I know what to do and not do. Also know they caught us red-handed. We're in big trouble. Cocaine is a powerful substance, keeps you holding on till the very last minute. Why didn't we start flushing as soon as we heard they were outside?

Dumb, that's all I feel right now. Brainless. Although experience insists there's no such thing as smart enough. Twenty minutes sooner or twenty minutes later there would've been no product here. It sucks. I'm sure the entire bust is my fault for selling from the house. Using makes you careless. No matter, there was no avoiding this. Sin has definite consequences.

The air in the caged patrol car is filled with whys and wherefores. Considered reasons for the search warrant take deep dives like bats in a dark, forsaken church house. I do my best to keep fright from latching on and sucking what's left of my body fluid. Still I'm ridiculed. Haunted by treacherous voices of accusation. My heart's entangled, my brain entrapped, and chaos attempts to asphyxiate me.

Busted.

19

TAKE THE KEYS

Take the key and lock her up,
Lock her up, Lock her up.
Take the key and lock her up,
My fair lady.

ilence. Other than the police radio, the trip downtown is perilously quiet. What is there to say? Can't even cry. Coop was taking a road trip so I got up much earlier than usual. Only slept two hours. I'm dog-tired, but no amount of exhaustion would welcome sleep. The patrol car pulls up to a huge garage-looking door. The officer mumbles some numbers over the intercom. The door rolls up, the car crawls in, and through beads of sweat the hair on my neck stands at attention.

What have I done? My babies, my babies. What will happen to my babies? Unconcerned and unaware of their welfare hours ago, now they're all I see.

The officer opens the back door and helps me from the car. Balance is tricky when your arms are unavailable. Two uniformed females with superior expressions start barking orders, while the driver searches the back seat.

"Turn around. Anything sharp in your pockets?" The arresting officer was kind enough to allow me to put on shorts, otherwise I'd be in a tiny little nightshirt.

"Step this way." Female officers are much more snooty than males.

Dry-mouthed with fear, I haven't said a word. Not "Yes, ma'am," not "Ok"—nothing. A huge electronic door closes behind me. Reminds me of a dump-truck bed settling into place after a trip to the landfill. Heavy steel that won't be budged. Discarded, caged, busted.

I'm escorted down a dirty hall and seated beside a sturdy folding table.

"Texas. Wow, is that your real name?"

Dumb question considering it's on a booking sheet. I nod. The nurse gives me the once over, takes my vital signs, and says, "Step on the scale, baby." The kindness in her voice makes my heart ache. "159 lbs." That's about what I weighed in high school and I've had three kids. Guess I'm thinner than I thought.

Next an intense, manly looking chick takes me to an area where I'm told to get undressed. They take my clothes from me and hand me something orange. I'm guessing it's an outfit but it feels more like paint tarp. I unravel the pants at top speed and attempt to get a leg in. It's cold and I'm not real interested in being some dike's eye-candy. Before my leg finds the other hole I hear.

"No, no, girl. You gotta squat and cough first."

"What's that?"

"Turn around spread your bum, squat and cough."

"You serious?"

"Do I look like I'm kidding?" She replies with a raised brow.

The clothing's stiff and rough. No bra or panties, an undergarment of despair is all I wear. The orange uniform is a sad sight but I've never found such joy in getting dressed. I'm led from that cove to a boxy holding cell. Locked there—alone and afraid.

Profane words and rude comments are chipped from the paint on the walls and carved into the wooden bench. Everything's bolted to the ground. I see why. Although I'm not a violent person, even I'd consider heaving something right about now. In an attempt to distract myself, I begin to read the graffiti. My eyes settle, and right there in the midst of the mess, I read it. Jesus. The dam of bewilderment bursts, flooding me with a rush of remorse.

Jesus, Jesus, what have I done? Please, Lord, help me. I'm sorry, I'm so sorry. In an instant my mind can see the old parsonage and the stare of my daddy's eyes as he explains to me what God did to secure my future. A scripture burns inside me. Repeating over and over. "Surely your sins will find you out." No help is found in these words and even in the midst of my deserved consequences I know this isn't my Savior's voice. He said this as a warning, not as an I told you so.

Buckets of fear pour over me. Soaked. Drowning in a pridefully crafted pit of self-sufficiency. Kinda like the Bible story of Joseph, only no-one tossed me into this hole. I jumped. But like Ole' Joe, I'm stuck. All I can do is wait. Wait and wonder.

Men in black ransacked my house and drug me away this morning. The trauma won't stop repeating in my head. Thank God the kids were at Bubba's. I stand in hopes that motion will generate new thought. I see an officer leading someone up the hallway. Is that Coop? It is. I lunge toward the door and bang with both fists. I hurl random questions his way—as if he can answer.

"Are you okay? What happened? What are we going to do? How do we get out of here?"

The officer hits the door with one swift move of his elbow. "Sit your ass down. That's what you're gonna do."

I turn and rest my back on the door. My limbs lose strength. I slide down the steel. Legs pulled to my chest, I drop my head and get back to crying. Hushed cries of self-despising embarrassment rise from a valley of useless regret. An empty, inky corner of entrapment I never knew existed. The cuffs are gone, still half my brain seems tied behind my back. Restricted. No clever one line rule, no glorious fame, not even an optimistic possibility ventures in to salvage me from my ruptured state.

I've gotta pee. There's a porcelain stool that's missing the seat, to my right. They can't expect me to pull down my pants in front of passing people. Most of them are guys. Isn't that against the law? I'll hold it.

A man a few doors down calls out. "Yo! What time's it gettin' to be, Nursy?"

"11:03 inmate." Comes her tiresome tone.

Drunken solos echo through moans of misery but attention surrenders when an argument explodes. I stand in time to see one girl wrestled to the ground, the other's knees are swiftly buckled from beneath her. Face down on the floor in seconds, they're cuffed and shackled. I'm alarmed yet unflinching. Grateful to be the only one in this cell.

I need out of here. What about my free call? Who will I call? My parents? My brothers? Mac! That's who. A bondsmen I sell to. He'll help.

"I haven't made a call either." I shout.

Thirty minutes pass before my cell door swings open. The officer points to a row of phones. "Make your call there and hurry it up."

I look at the list posted on wall and find Mac's number. I hold my breath. It's ringing. He answers. Recognizing my broken voice he says, "Don't worry, Tex, I'm lookin' out. You ain't got no bond yet. I'll be there when ya do."

"Thank you, Mac. My god, thank you."

I hang up and an officer returns me to my cell. On the way back I sweetly ask, "Can I use the bathroom?"

"You don't see that toilet stool, girl? That's the only bathroom you'll be using here. Better get busy."

"But people can see me," I urge.

"Don't like it? Don't come to jail." Without concern he flips forward the heavy door behind me. Crash. It closes with a confidence that would make Rambo flinch.

Hours die like struggling gnats on flypaper. By the time two plain-clothes detectives stop outside my door, fatigue from my mental fight for resolution has demolished me.

"Open five." The lock pops and the door swings out. "This way, Stready."

Once seated I take note of the room. Wooden desk. Padded chairs. I know what's coming. They throw around names, ask questions, but get no response.

"Neva talk. De'll twis' it all ta hell." It's been 11 years since I've laid eyes on Mr. Jackson. Still his laws preach truth in my memory like a Bible-beating missionary. Everything I say is well edited. On and on they ask. Things I know. Things I don't know. For the most part my entire mind seems absent.

After what seems like eternity, a middle-aged woman officer, with raspberry hair enters the room joking with the guys. "She's done, fellas. Enough's enough. Let me have her." Her mannerism brings a sense of comfort.

"Texas Stready. Now that's a name if I ever heard one. Come on Miss Texas, let's go." Down a long corridor we walk. Each step echoes from ceiling to wall and back again. "You'll be housed in 3-D. That's my unit. I'm there five days a week. This your first time?"

"Yes, ma'am."

"Some pretty serious charges, Ms. Stready."

"Thanks for the reminder."

She snaps her head my way with a puzzled look and begins to laugh. I can't contain my sigh of relief.

"I like you, Ms. Texas. You speak your mind. That's a good thing in here."

We enter what they call the sally-port. (As many times as I've graced these halls you'd think I'd know why—I don't.) The back door closes before the door to the front opens. She points to the floor, "Grab your matt and box. Everything you get's in there. Commissary's on Monday. You'll figure things out as you go. If you have a question come to the LCC. The Lock Control Center, that is." She points towards the darkly tinted plexiglass. "I'll be in there."

"You're on the upper level. Cell fourteen. There's no one in there. Not yet. So get set up and enjoy the time to yourself while you can." And just like that she's gone.

I stand inside the entrance in a stupor. Astonishment. Not the good kind. The trumpet of drug-induced insomnia blaring in my ear is hushed by a soft stream of continuous chatter.

"Texas?" I make eye contact but there's no recognition.

"There are 28 cells in D-Dorm, most of the girls are housed here fourteen cells on top and fourteen on bottom—two bunks each cell—you're in the last cell on the upper level and everyone wants that one, there's nobody in it and that's a good thing, dinner's at 4:30, you have to have your bed made by then." Her continuous flow of words are a waste, still I follow her lead.

Each cell door's swung open. There's no plexiglass on them like the ones downstairs. They have real bars. Old, rusty, real bars. Various attitudes and ethnic backgrounds echo between like-dressed women. My outfit makes me one of them. Washed-out faces are clustered like grapes across this crowded yet hollow space. Three rows of stairs ascend to the top-tier. The last set leads right to my doorway. As if they'd been expecting me.

"I'll grab your stuff, just come this way," says my over-informative tagalong. "I can set up your cell, I'm good at it, been here three times this year, why'd they bring you to Collier County's Finest?"

I don't answer. Not even a thank you. It takes all I have left to remain focused on the direction of the black fourteen stenciled on the wall. My last brush with peace is found shortly after I enter my 9x5 cell. The clamor of unfamiliar voices intensifies my sense of alienation.

"I'm straight. I got it." Grabbing the lumpy green mattress I dismiss my helper from her self-appointed responsibility.

Across the steel plank that juts from the concrete wall, I toss the mat. I collapse onto my bunk, without even the search for a sheet to cover with. Tears zoom in, heavy sobs chasing them. A fierce fight to keep my senses from shutdown gives way to a careless and ignorant area of calm. Sleep. I awake throughout the night in a panic. Almost as if I'm being choked.

Trapped.

20

WHEN SKIES ARE GRAY

You are my sunshine,
My only sunshine.
You make me happy,
When skies are grey.
You'll never know dear,
How much I love you.
Please don't take my sunshine away.

A rude rattle awakens me and truth slaps me in the jaw.

My god, I am in jail.

"It's third chow call, Stready. Better be standing at your door tomorrow morning or you won't be eating." The officer shoves a school lunch tray through a thin slot in the bars splashing what looks like watery oatmeal over my hand.

"Okay," I mumble scratching my head in confusion. "Can I use the phone?"

She continues along the balcony calling back to me, "Not now, girl. It's chow time."

"What time *is* it? As a matter of fact, what day is it?"

"Sunday, 4:30 a.m. I'm done with questions, Stready. You're lucky I answered those."

I stand at the locked door looking out into the vacant space below. I don't know what to expect or how to react. My brain's still trapped.

The beige tray in my hand is hardly warm. Each compartment holds things that resemble food but the smell has no allure. My innards throb with a sorrowful ache of uncertainty. Talk about a shift in circumstance. I'm not the boss-lady here. Nothing's normal or even familiar. Thoughts are choppy, opposing what's left of my right mind.

My stiff bones moan. Weighty sleep and lack of narcotics are a strong cocktail to get down. Wonder how long it's been since I slept this hard or woke without cocaine? Many months. Many, many, months. The stream of existence I've been wading in has engulfed me. I'm drowning.

"Texas, you up? It's me, Lil Bit, from in-town. You don't want you tray, push it dis-a-way? To the lef'."

"Do what? I definitely don't want this crap."

"Jus slide it unda da door, an push it to the lef'. Here, see my hand?" A chubby brown arm reaches toward the base of my door.

"Yah, I see you. Man, you've gained some serious weight. From eating this junk?"

"Don't be talkin' trash, gurl. You be gobblin' it up 'fore ya kno it. Watch what I say. Lessin' you get commissary. If ya do, I want ya trays. K?"

"Just get this. We'll see about the rest. When do they let us out? I need to make a call."

"Later, dat's when. Like everything else here. Later. You may as well lay back down. Door's don't pop till seven and phones ain't on till eight. Look straight from ya door, da clock's above the LCC. See?"

I look at the time then turn. With two short steps I'm back at the bed. I sit down, careful not to bang my head on the bunk above. Bunkbeds and tall people don't get along. I lean down and open my supply box. There's a discolored blanket that feels like a cheap cotton ball inside. I woke up with my skin stuck to the plastic mat. Now that same sweat has me freezing. I stretch the scratchy blanket over me, shifting about to find a spot without bumps. Not exactly cozy but better than cold.

A loud popping sound vibrates through the room. My door swings open. I sit up to find a shamefaced, stringy white lady—with too many freckles and too much forehead—standing in my doorway.

"Today's our chore day but I got you. I know how much the first week blows." She gently closes my door with a smile.

"I have no clue what that means, but thanks," I say covering my head with what feels like a potato sack and turning my back on reality. Didn't get much sleep at home. Too much to be up to there—if you know what I mean.

Before inner voices begin to taunt me with blame or hazard, I'm gone. Lost in snores of neglect.

All I do is cry. Sleep or cry. Thank goodness there's no physical withdrawal from cocaine, otherwise I'd be a sick puppy. Don't get me wrong. I'm sick. Sick in the head. The longer I'm awake the more I realize it.

I was arrested once at sixteen for shoplifting but never made it downtown. Then at nineteen I was picked up for an unpaid traffic ticket and got as far as holding. Now the charges are trafficking cocaine, possession of marijuana with intent to sell, and possession of drug paraphernalia. Trafficking has nothing to do with a car, it's about the amount. It carries a minimum mandatory of three to five years in the Florida State Penitentiary.

Mad remorse echoes through me. Despair is an overpowering beast that's happy to gnaw on any brain space available.

I convince myself to chill. Don't want blowout to land me in medical housing. Heard some folks in holding talking about it. Sounded even worse than this.

If I go to prison, Azlynn will be thirteen, Jordan eleven, and Justice nine when I'm released. Doesn't seem real. Almost a week and I'm still here. The cops are happy to have captured the white girl named Texas. Been charging through town partying and selling dope for thirteen years now. My bond is $140,000. Ridiculous. It's my first charge.

"That's a whole lot of dead presidents, Texas. Sorry man, I jus' can't stand it." That's what the bondsman says when I finally get through to him. They took my cash in the raid. He's got to make a living. And me? I'm broke.

My parents have never had money. They wouldn't do it if they did. I'd never ask them anyway. I did what it took to get here, so here I am. Not a snitch either. Such a disgraceful role. Why should someone else take the rap for my wrong moves? Jo-Jo always said, "Everyone hates a snitch."

Request forms are taken and supplies given each morning at 7:30 a.m. You have to have one, to get one. In other words, if you want a new toothbrush or comb you must turn in your old one. To get toilet paper you need the empty roll. My tears take me through a roll a day and I'm not too crazy about mornings. Bob Barker is the name of the manufacturer who produces these poorly made items; guess the price is right.

This place is insane and the cops get a kick out of it. The LCC is tinted but through the shadowed glass they laugh and point, as if watching some Steve Martin movie.

Razors and tweezers are given two days a week—at supply call—and only for an hour. I'm sure you can picture what Tuesdays and Thursdays are like. Fifteen females fighting for the one good shower. The other ten waiting in line to use the metal telephone as a mirror to pluck eyebrows or chin hair. Pathetic. One set of sorry tweezers sure can cause a heap of trouble. When fights break out we lose hair removal privileges for the week. A tense, high wire act of nervous pandemonium.

Mail Call is every day about 2 p.m. That's when they hand out mail and return answered request forms. I got my Bible today from the chaplain. Saturday's church service was great. New Hope Ministries does it. That's the church my mom's worked at for 7 years. Grant Thigpen's the pastor. He married me and dedicated Azlynn and Jordan. I attended church there regularly when my marriage was together—if together's what you call it. Bubba and I sang in the choir. Azlynn even sang a solo in the Christmas cantata one year.

Pastor Grant's a big bear of a man. Not a teddy bear—cute and full of fluff—more like a grizzly who loves people. He's not scary or dangerous, just straightforward with no apologies. Being taught and loved by this man healed years of confused turmoil brought on by spiritual abuse. I love him almost as much as I do my own daddy.

The ladies from the women's ministry Mother led, now come to the jail to remind Christian inmates of the God who loves them anyway. It's such a relief to see them. Ms. Sherry's so happy you'd think I'd sat up in my casket. I don't get how any of it's possible. If I was God, I would have been done with me a long time ago. There's no doubt where I went wrong. I turned to something besides Him for help. The Bible clearly teaches that Christ is always around wanting to give us new insight. Why am I so bullheaded?

Yesterday's gone. I need to move on from it. I'm not going to resort to drugs anymore. Everyone who loves me is so tired. The thing they don't realize is I'm way more tired than they could ever be. Just think, I'm stuck with me all the time.

Thirteen unlucky days of savagery I've spent here. Awful. And no news of my case. Not facts. The girls have a host of answers that all end in maybe. Jailhouse lawyers. Chicks who have been here so much they can tell you what's going to happen. At least that's what they promise. Truth told, you never know for sure.

I'm tired of talk but silence is scarce. Lockdown is after meals. Everyone falls asleep then. For some reason we've been locked in our individual cells for two hours today. No explanation. Turns out quiet can be just as noisy. I would shave my head or give up a finger to hug my babies right now.

I hear the sally-port door roll open. A flood of chatter fills the dayroom as the girls return from recreation. A hand full of them scamper to the base of my stairwell and shout up with strange exuberance.

"Texas, Texas! Eddie Cooper's window's on the Rec Yard. He told us to tell you to come to recreation from now on."

I rush to my door "You saw Coop?" Flutters of energy dash about my intestines and quiver inside my eyeballs. "Where? How? When do we go again? When?"

"Tuesday. Sometimes at 8 a.m., sometimes at 8 p.m."

"You guys have to make sure I'm up. Please. Do you hear me? Please make sure I go." Back in my room I plop down on the bed, smile so gigantic it makes my cheeks ache.

My new bunky raises her head. Margaret. She's a sketchy older lady with long red hair, a pointy nose, and sharp eyes. She's not as mean as she looks. Beating her daughter's what got her here. Talk is, you couldn't even see the twelve year old's eyes. No telling. This place is gossip central. She knows the system. I'll give her that much.

She explains to me how the guys housing unit faces the Rec Yard. "Although the clouded window's as thin as your face is wide, you can hear each other. Only-thing-is, if you get caught you go straight to the hole."

"Jail is jail," I say rolling my eyes. "I'll never miss another Rec. Not only that, I'll sing the entire time I'm in the hole, if only I can hear his voice."

A warm sense of reassurance melts through me like chocolate in the middle of a s'more. But in an instant the goodness is gone, as if handed over to an eager child. Replaced by the agony that tags alongside a five day wait. An eternity. No bellyaching from me. At least it's something to look forward to.

Having a man around has kept me alive since I left home. Drugs, money, attention. That's what brought light. But this gloomy forecast has taken my overcast mentality to a whole new level.

Ominous.

21

DOWN CAME THE RAIN

The itsy bitsy spider climbed up the waterspout.
Down came the rain
and washed the spider out.
Out came the sun
and dried up all the rain,
and the itsy bitsy spider climbed up the spout again.

The food here sucks. A starchy pile of day old carbohydrates. Most of the so-called meat is processed soybeans. Horrible. Mom's putting money in my account on Thursday. Then I'll be able to order. What would I do without Mom? She always believes for the best. She can tell I'm serious or she'd never do this.

Chips and candy will be my diet come commissary day. No wonder people get fat here—they do nothing and eat everything. The food hounds will do your chores if you give them your trays. Already got that in place. But I'd instantly give it all up for a chance to hug my Momma.

Through the phone I hear relief and enthusiasm in her speech. This excites me. She shows far more emotion on this end of the spectrum. Please don't think for a moment my mother doesn't love me. She does. Tells everyone when I'm doing well. Everyone but me.

This life is over. Done. Finally learned my lesson.

Saturday's church service is great. I forgot how good it feels to be in God's presence. Girls in the dorm keep asking me to pray with them. After lockdown each night they yell out, "Pray, Texas. Pray." Don't feel worthy. Outrageous how God keeps forgiving me, but He does.

★ ★ ★

Today's the day. I wait by the huge steel door dressed in a borrowed, white Tee and my stiff orange pants. Recreation is the only time you can wear your whites out of the dorm. It's Tuesday morning, time to go outside and talk to my baby. This whole ordeal has shaken me beyond anything I've ever experienced.

The sky outside is ominous. Doesn't bother me any. My time's spent leaning into the narrow, clouded window. Listening to Coop's every sigh and shuffle feels like the greatest event of my life. We got lucky. Today the officer in the tower doesn't care if the girls talk in the windows. I talk and laugh, cry and question. This man really loves me. I know it.

Jail has a manner of shining new light on old lies. I have an intense desire to tell him the truth about the crack. I'm guilty and ashamed. But I can't do it. It would be wrong to add more disappointment to his already burdensome state. What if the paperwork says something to prove it? I can't. Won't risk him abandoning me. Not here, not now. I'll think of something if it comes up.

I can picture the joy that lights his kind eyes when I say something crazy that makes him laugh. I love to do that. Always have. But with him it's more fun than usual—especially in here.

"Line up ladies. We're headin' in," comes the racket from the guard tower.

"I love you. I love you." I yell towards the window until I hear the exit door pop. Man oh man, how will I live till Thursday?

Brief moments of calm are quickly invaded by alarming concern. I'm facing prison. Scary. Two months have passed since that fateful day. Bubba has agreed to bring the kids. I make it through most days anymore without tears and today I'm on top of the world. Ecstatic at the thought of seeing them.

At 6:45 p.m. they call my name. Bubba's really here. Can't believe it. The officer leads me and five other girls down the hallway. He places us each in separate booths. A steel stool is seated in a cove. A black phone hangs to the right. Thick hard plastic is between my seat and the opposite one. The place my children will be any minute now.

My heart skips when I hear the door on that side roll open. Talking and laughing. I can hear their small inquisitive voices getting closer. How do I explain? What will I say? Three little heads with spirals of coco brown hair and smiles that outshine the North Star leave me breathless. They point, yell, and struggle for the phone.

Humiliation and pain spin circles through my entire body, as if someone pressed the purée button on a blender. A grinding, growling, gritty sound turns me inside out. I want to puke. Be strong, I tell myself but accusation corners me hard when I hear his precious voice.

"Mommy, Mommy. It's Mommy," Jordan shouts.

Their dad picks up the phone. I can hardly inhale. Thoughts of this incarceration being a minimum of three years, is more than I can stomach. He lowers the speaker to their ears.

"Hi, my babies. My babies, I love you guys. I'm so sorry." Quickly calming myself, I begin to ask important kids' stuff. Questions I've been remiss in asking for months. "How do you like your teacher? Who's your best friend? Are french fries still your favorite food?"

Before the visit ends, Bubba lifts the phone to his embittered face. Like a stadium of excited basketball fans, disgrace erupts. I've shut tight the door to our relationship and it remains sealed. Can't remember the good. Vicious blame-packed grenades fly between us.

"Can't believe you did this. You're stupid. This is better than life with me? You're in jail, Texas, and you're going to prison. Prison! I'm filing for custody of my children."

Animosity and defense accumulate like rain in a rock pit. The downpour of hurt splashes hard causing a dangerous shift. You know what they say, "never go swimming in a rock pit."

"Yeah, cause you're such a great dad. You've never been involved, you asshole, and now you're the Greatest American Hero? Mr. Mom or somebody? Don't waste my time or your money. Bring me the paper I'll sign them over to you. It's high time you stand up. Be a real man."

Insults and innuendos thrust through the phone like daggers and in a split second of hysterical rage I slam the receiver down. "Officer, I want to go back." I stand to walk away but am crippled by the look on their faces. I grab the phone and in a tragic moment of lost reality, I see my children wiping their eyes as they fade away through freedom's door. I beat and beat on the plastic until an officer triangles my elbow behind me.

"Do I need cuffs, Stready? Visitation's over anyway. Let's go."

I cry all the way back to the dorm and throughout the next few days. Before this marriage, I was not a reactor. I use to pride myself on my ability to remain calm. Must have been another life.

After supply call, I've started a morning Bible study. Slept right through it today. Crying tends to wreck you like that.

Time builds tolerance—but in the meantime, in-between time—jailhouse remedies have saved my life. Unintelligible shouts over the blaring intercom didn't even disturb my sleep, thanks to moist biscuit bread knotted in cellophane and shoved down my ear canal. At first, the volcano-like rumble of a flushing toilet jolted me throughout the night. Now my sleep is unaffected.

A Maxipad mask blocks the overhead light that's positioned to shine directly into your face all night. When I tie it to my head I can't help but sing, "This is the night the lights went out in Georgia." It's perfect. Cause the next line speaks of an innocent man and everybody in jail's innocent, you know.

"Hey Stready, it's lunch time." The officer calls as she passes my cell. "You guys are going outside at 1:00 today instead of 7:00. I'm sure you'll be wantin' to talk to your little boyfriend, so get up." I smile. Miss Cruz. She's my favorite officer.

At one o'clock we crowd the sally-port and assume the position. Mrs. Dudley always says the exact same thing. "You know the drill, girls. Legs spread, hands on the wall." Then comes the search.

Except for the people in lockdown, the entire jail uses the same Rec Yard. I'm forever amazed by the items that make it from the cellblock. Bars of soap to write messages on the cement. Prewritten notes without signatures. Hard candy to suck on. Bras and panties to leave for husbands or boyfriends. Frightening to consider where they keep these treasures to avoid being sent back during pat-down. No two ways around it, criminals are ingenious people.

I skip past the window and tap my fingers. Today's officer's a jerk, so I gotta keep it moving. Second lap I call out, "Ed. Eddie. Coop, it's me." Can't stand around waiting for a response so I walk on pretending to exercise. When I pass again I press my ear as close to the window as space allows.

"Coop bonded, gurl. Las' night. So don't be bangin' on this window no mo. Not less you gone try to show me sum luv."

My eyes pop open, like a raccoon caught pilfering a picnic basket. I take another lap, heart pounding faster than my feet. "You sure?" I ask when I make it back.

"He my bunky. I was here when they tol' him ta pac' it up."

My middle buckles and I strain for oxygen as if blasted by a rocketing dodgeball. I fall to my knees shake my head and wail. Wouldn't wish here on anybody I care for, but what will I do without him? What?

I'm not going anywhere. It would take fourteen thousand to get me out. I have a bond reduction hearing in three weeks but who knows what will happen there. Talking to him twice a week and mail each day is what enabled me to hold on. Now what? Is he at his parent's house? I don't remember their phone number.

A handful of girls huddle around me in reassurance. It's no help. My comfort's gone. It vanished. Left the building with inmate #54725.

On the 7th, I turn thirty and Jordan's six. Never miss our birthday celebration. Sad. The next twenty days are furious. Wicked even. At last the calendar comes to rest on Thursday November 27th, 1997. It's 7:30 a.m. and I'm in line for court. Hope they lower my bond.

When I enter the courtroom, my parents, a group of church members, and some life-long family friends sit on the front row. My teeth start to chatter and it's not even cold. First time in front of the judge. Everyone's been praying but none more than me.

Shouts of praise go up when Judge Clark announces my new bond amount. Coop has me home that same night. If I was unsure of my love for this man—and I wasn't—there's no question of it tonight. Dripping with total appreciation.

Drenched.

22

TUMBLING AFTER

Jack and Jill went up the hill,
To fetch a pail of water.
Jack fell down and broke his crown,
And Jill came tumbling after

"Your lunch for tomorrow is packed. I'm going to bring it to you."

"I don't need it, Tex. I'm good."

"Don't try to talk me out of it. I want to see you, Coop. Kiss you, take care of you. You have a job now and that means I have one too. I'm on my way." I insist.

Okay, so I'm a little obsessed when it comes to Eddie. Been home for three months awaiting court. Divorce is shifty business, not having my children is a stunner, and the hazard of prison is staggering. I no longer own my identity. I cling to the only thing I can get my hands on—Coop.

He has a seven month old baby from another girl. The two of them were finished before we met but she was already four months pregnant. This adds to my uncertainty and so does not living together. However, the A#1 reason for my attachment is guilt. I've always enjoyed a self-established confidence but now my conscience is calculating life from a place of disgrace. Drenched in insecurity. A stranger to myself.

My mother's aggravation tells me I'm over-doing it. Still I load the cooler and jump in my Mazda, headed his way. As much as I'd like to recount for you the exact events of the evening, I can't. We argue and I rip from the driveway in a fit of anger. Smash!

Salvaged from the car, I'm air-vac'd to the next county. I wake in the Lee Memorial Trauma Center and eight days have passed. Seems like the chopper ride to the hospital left part of my brain on the scene. I'm confused. Not sure what's going on.

Happy to report I do recognize my children when Bubba brings them to see me. But not much else. I keep asking him misplaced questions. "Why are you acting like this? You're not hugging me, are you mad? Don't you love me anymore?" He says nothing.

My sister-in-law, Dorothy, can't stand the indirect deception. She urges him to be honest. "You can't pretend like everything's okay. It's not right, Bubba. Tell her the truth." He hesitates in hopes of a fresh start but in the end determines she's right.

"We weren't together before this accident, Texas. You're with a guy named Eddie."

Not enough sense to consider his heart, I blurt out. "Oh yeah. Where is Coop?"

The next details must be repeated to you as they were described to me. I was t-boned on the driver's side by a sheriff's car that was in a hurry. The ambulance driver tells me he knew I'd have no legs when he arrived on the scene.

"When you've been the first respondent to as many accidents as I have, you know what to expect from looking at the car. You were sitting straight up in the passenger seat. This made me sure your legs were severed. Otherwise, the center console would've forced you sideways. Instead, it was as if someone had picked you up and set you in the passenger seat."

God spared my life. For sure. The street had no traffic light and a ten second blind spot, due to a small bridge. The officer was speeding with no overhead lights flashing. My trafficking charge was dropped to possession with intent and I was given three years probation. Got approved for disability. First round. I suppose I'll never have the specifics of this outcome. Suffice it to say the system can be prejudiced. Cruel to outsiders and lenient towards its own.

A common statement in recovery meetings or programs is this. "You won't change until you've hit bottom." I thought jail was it. Guess not. Looks like bottom's hit me.

All I do is ask for Eddie. I ask until my parents tell him it's okay to come. I'm not wise to the fact that they've asked him to stay away. They've never been real crazy about the thought of him and me. This situation's just one more reason.

Tested positive for cocaine at the hospital. When Mother asked the trauma doctor if they tested me for drugs, he replied, "She lit up the charts." Addiction's a beast. As bad as I felt about my lies to Coop, I was still unable to say no when someone offered me a line.

Thrilled to see him when he comes. Takes us ten minutes to get through the mushy stuff. When Coop can't hold back any longer, he backs away from my bedside and with a sad look on his face he asks. "You use cocaine, Boo?"

Stunned in disbelief, I lay pinned to the bed by shame. Humiliated. I push out my chin and nod a yes in his direction.

Next comes, "and crack? Were you smoking crack before we got popped, Tex?"

No clue how he knows but I can't lie. He deserves the truth. I shake my head again. For a moment he stares as if impaired by his own traumatic brain injury. Difference is, he's able to walk away from his hurt. And he does.

"No, Coop. Wait. Please don't leave. Please!" His stride is steady, without relent. I should've told him when we were in jail. What have I done? The love of my life is leaving. Gone forever.

I yell and scream at the top of my lungs. I spring from the bed is if I can stand but meet the cold terrazzo floor head-on. Nurses charge in to restore my IV, return me to bed, and administer a sedative. Shouts of hysteria lower to moans, then whimpers. Drugs rush in to save the day once more.

The neurologist is dumbfounded when I go to his office a month later. No wheelchair, already on a walker. He gathers his staff together and asks, "Do you know who this is? Texas Stready! This is Texas Stready," he announces. "Mrs. Stready, we never thought you'd be normal."

My response comes, "Doc, I wasn't real normal in the first place so no one will notice." Everyone laughs.

Now that I'm home, Coop tries to forgive. Bubba and him get into a huge argument outside my parent's house one day. This seals the deal. It's over and who can blame the man. A trafficking charge, a lying drug-addicted girlfriend, witnessing a horrible car accident where he thought I was dead. Now a crazed ex. The end.

This thrusts me into a zone as alien as outer space. An unfamiliar area that lacks life's usual certainties. Things are backwards. Cross-eyed.

The next three years are splattered through my skull like misfired buckshot. I'm not myself. No restraint, regard, or remorse. I'm "off the chain," as they say in the hood.

Wounded body parts allow for powerful medication and Medicaid foots the bill. Now my drugs are free—and legal. Logic is loose, shaken that way by the impact it seems. The sense of disorder, accompanied by permanent edginess, is far more excruciating than my pain. One 10mg Percocet removes the daggers, two makes my skin fit, and three restores humor. For a while.

Cocaine's not like pills. Gets you high each time but there's never enough. With pills it takes more and more to get you there, making the race the same speed only in a different direction.

Car rides are upsetting, until my first trip to Walgreens. Commitment to the cause keeps sudden scares away and a squeamish stomach can be ignored. My brother Curtis' wife, Nicole, doesn't work and she's a partier too. Not like me but we're pals. She knows how to keep her mouth shut. My parents don't want me on all these narcotics.

As soon as the car pulls from the drive-through, I wreck the stapled sack and dismantle the amber container. I forgot my water. Oh well. I count out twelve, hand her two, and toss the other ten into my mouth. The chalky crunch ushers in a pick-me-up long before the true effects settle in.

"Texas, how on earth do you do that?" she questions with a sour expression.

"Just do it. Thought they'd suck without water but they're not so bad." Desire waves its magic wand and transforms unheard-of into doable.

★ ★ ★

Home and high aren't a good blend. Especially with a broken heart. I call Coop. A lot. But he's disappeared. Gone from home and lost to me. He checks in every once in a while, almost as if he wants to get over it. But he can't. I feel like a dinosaur that's been mysteriously transported to the 21st Century. Things have changed. They'll never be the same. As much as I hate it, it's true.

I grab for high in hopes of indifference but it won't show up. The call of the wild begins to howl my name. The clamor of the streets will be a great distraction.

My mind is ruptured, that's plain to see. I burst into tears in the middle of sentences; can't remember what I'm saying. Without notable cause, an eerie feeling darts in and surrounds me many times throughout the day. It's as if I'm midpoint—in a one-way tunnel—with a semi barreling straight for me. Fear's only a fraction of it. A convoy of nameless other emotions are equally disruptive. They lurk around in the darkness just shy of comprehension. Hate it.

These dynamics bring new appreciation to the Coyote's struggle. That darn Road Runner sure is elusive. Not sure which way's up or how I'll get there. Can't stay down here, not even if they expect me to.

Fallen.

23

TIP ME OVER

I'm a little teapot
Short and stout,
Here is my handle
Here is my spout.
When I get all steamed up
Hear me shout,
Just tip me over and pour me out!

Nothing's off limits. Been up for days shooting crack rock. It was powder last week but lately there's no good dust available. The rush from this is super intense. Vinegar or lemon juice on a piece of crack breaks it down to a liquid you can draw up and shoot. Wonder what junkie figured this out. The high is just as brief as it is intense. You have to shoot an entire twenty piece to feel anything. And I do mean anything. I can get three or four good ear-ringers off smoking a twenty, but right now the needle has me entranced. What can I say, I'm in mainline mode. It bees like that sometimes.

Yesterday I ran 90 units. An enormous blast. I ended up in the neighbor's back yard sprawled beneath a lawn chair. My imagination produced a cop across the street watching me through binoculars. Disturbing. Wally and his girl were so busy with their own stuff, they didn't notice me leave. When I return they're searching the canal. Thought I'd fallen in.

"What are you guys doing?" I say as I walk into the back-yard. "I'm right here. Let's go inside and get high. I got stash. I'll share."

I'm staying at Wallace's place. He's a kind man who loves having me around. He was awarded a huge settlement years ago. When he got the money he bought this beautiful home for his mom. She's gone-on now, leaving him alone to do as he pleases here.

The yard is immaculate. The front room has white sofas custom-fitted with thick plastic covers. Every figurine and stat-ute are where she left them. A perfect decoy.

The master bedroom's a different story. It was once as pretty as the rest of the house. Now the dressers have cigarette burns surrounded by miscellaneous papers and drug paraphernalia. The carpet's grungy. Worn to the pad in spots. The sheets are discolored and lack the elastic to hold them in place. Not a city crack-house, a Naples dope hole. If you got cash and nowhere to do your drugs—as long as you're willing to share—this is the place to be.

Violated probation again. Tomorrow's court. It's been ten months since the accident but I haven't talked to my folks in weeks. I'm not the type to hang around making up stories. Once I'm using I hightail it out of there.

If I can make it to their place, I'll get to court. Otherwise, I may fall asleep and be lost for ten hours. That's what happens if you only sleep when forced. Even if I am up, who would drive me? Better start walking. Wait around here any longer and dope's sure to show up. It always does. Then I'll be caught up.

I have a nice shot left. I'll save it till I get to my parents as motivation to keep walking. The house is at least three miles from here. Out the door and down the street I travel. It's 2 a.m. and the cops in Golden Gate are funny. Don't like late nighters. They may not know my face but the name is unforgettable. And name's the first question they ask.

After 40 minutes I see the driveway. I had to stop and rest. A few times. The trip took forever. My shirt's glued to me by sweat. Mascara oozes into my eyes causing them to burn and make more of a mess. I'm sure I look like someone who escaped from a creature feature flick. Track marks run up and down both arms, hands, legs. Kept a tan all my life trying to look related to my children. Now I haven't seen the sun in weeks— kids either. Jail-time, the hospital, and this lifestyle have me gaunt and pasty.

"Dammit, the door's locked." I wiggle at one of the jalousies. If I can get it loose enough I'll reach in and unlock the garage door. Tension's turned a corner in my mind and irrational's closing in on me. I feel like breaking the window.

Have I mentioned I'm not a social cocaine addict? Not anymore. Since the accident I get even more freaked out. Best to ask me a yes or no question if you're expecting an answer. Too uneasy to talk, I become frozen by nervous considerations of every type.

Conflict with the door is more than I can handle. I need my last shot but it's dark out here. Like a burglar I tiptoe a few houses down. The glow of a streetlamp directs me to a good vein. Don't want to miss my last shot. When I see headlights or hear a car engine I lean back into the shadows.

This is not good. Shooting up under a streetlamp on a main road? Not good at all. But cocaine's never learned to take a No. A self-existent, pushy, and irrational god who owns my world.

It revolves slowly and solely around itself, and is sure to run you down if you take too long or get in its way.

My rig's old. The needle's bent from overuse. Gotta be careful. I've heard stories of needles breaking off, shooting through the vein, and puncturing the heart. Who knows if it's true. Addicts love to tell gory tales. I poke around in the bend of my arm trying to register a vein. I pullback slowly to check the condition of the needle. It's gone. Oh my god!

I try to calm myself thinking the faster my heart beats the sooner it will explode. After two or three long minutes, logic's door slides open and relief moseys in. I know how long it takes for the blood in my arm to make it to my brain. Can't take that much longer to get to the heart. I'm okay.

I move from the light and dig through my purse in search of a different point. No luck. I shoot the contents of the syringe into my mouth then flick the tool into the street. At least it's in my system and not on the ground.

Frustration's chained to my neck. I drag it back to my parents and push it out of view long enough to finagle my way into the garage. I try the inside door handle. It's bolted. I'm scared to jiggle too loud. Don't want to get shot. Dad has a good ear and loves his guns.

Between a wide spectrum of various items, I notice a desk chair. It's padded and swivels. Nice and comfortable. I sit down, lean back, and prop up my feet. The heat's unbearable. Sweltering. I roll the chair outside next to the air conditioning compressor. The air it blows isn't cool but it's better than nothing.

"Texas! What are you doing? Wake up!" my dad demands.
Through squinted eyes I ask. "What time is it?"

"7:50 on Tuesday morning. What are you doing here?"

Daylight, accompanied by Dad's agitated tone, awakens thought life. "I need some clothes and a ride to the courthouse. I have court this morning at 9."

After I get dressed Dad takes me to the courthouse. I raise my arm to flip through the posted docket. I notice my tailored suit hanging from my frail frame. Shabby. Before now, not appearing to be a drug addict was of the utmost importance. I realize people know the truth. Just don't want to fuel their gossip, in protection of my young'uns. Too little caution to worry with that these days.

Can't keep my eyes open. "If you fall asleep in here one more time, you'll be held in contempt. Got it, ma'am?" the bailiff advises. I fiddle around on the bench trying to appear alert. Miraculously I make it till my name is called. Proving willpower a most worthy ally.

I stand, hands behind my back and perform an outstanding plea for mercy. The judge sentences me to 60 days and gives me until the following Monday to turn myself in. A court official escorts me to the probation office to give them record of my sentence.

On the way down, for some unknown reason, I decide to tell her how glad I am to have this extra time. "I need to go to the hospital and get this needle removed from my arm." I push back my sleeve exposing the swollen area.

The elevator slides open. As I attempt to step forward she extends her arm and says, "Wait just one minute." Without hesitation she pushes the Up button. When we arrive on Floor Three, she marches my happy ass right back into the courtroom. There, I'm promptly taken into custody. Shackled, cuffed, and escorted via ambulance from Collier County Jail to Naples Community Hospital.

At times exhaustion comes in handy. Brief intervals is all I know of my hours spent at NCH. I'm grateful. Cuts down on the embarrassment of public incarceration. Then there's the needle embedded in my arm—not exactly something you want broadcasted.

The foreign object's removed and I'm returned to the medical housing unit of the CCJ.

Flattened.

24

ROUND AND ROUND

The wheels on the bus go
round and round,
round and round,
round and round.
The wheels on the bus go
round and round,
all through the town!

When you stay out of it as much as I do, reality sucks. Jail. Seems like the exact same people are standing in the exact same places. No pointing at black kettles, I'm here too. They moved me back to regular housing. What a relief. The people in the medical dorm have real mental issues. They stay mad at nurses, neighbors, even ghosts. One lady spread her own feces on the wall. Stunk for hours. Thank goodness we have individual cells down there.

Church is today. Wonder if the ladies from New Hope still come. How embarrassing. I deserve to be here but I can't believe I am. I was serious when I promised to never come back. Can't even trust myself.

Being behind a locked door brings focus to what matters. Sharp and intense as if x-ray vision's been activated. Only there's no superhero soaring in to save the day.

My kids. I've only seen them for isolated moments in the last months. Heartless. How do you find yourself flattened into a corner where nothing matters? Not sure, but I'm here. Stuck in what feels like a shrinking triangle.

Will they send me to prison this time? Calculating the odds is mind-blowing, so I gather my thoughts and head for the previous subject. Church. A Bible passage comes to mind. It speaks of being hot or cold and tells that God will spit you from His mouth if you're lukewarm. Without full understanding of this verse, I figure hot seemed impossible so I chose cold. Made sense to me.

"Line up, churchgoers," the officer shouts.

When I walk into the meeting room, Ms. Sherry hugs me like it's my wedding day. Shame gouges at my conscience. I'm sickened by the thought of me. Nauseated by the marks on my exterior and offended with my weak-minded interior.

Praise and worship is powerful. I can feel the presence of God, although I don't know why He'd want to be near me. I listen intently to every word spoken. Off in the distance hope waves at me. It shines a light in my direction but fear of further disappointment keeps me in the dark.

Being locked-up is rough but no doubt what's best. When choice is removed I'm left with the sandpaper of truth. It's harsh but necessary. Smooths things out. I suppose it's preparation for the final finish. The Bible tells me, God always finishes what He starts. Wish He'd hurry it up.

Released on probation—again. Mom agrees to let me move home. I love her so much, she never gives up. Poor Mom. Too bad she got stuck with me for a daughter.

Time passes taking with it my appreciation. I'm bored and lazy. I suppose I can eat all the Lucky Charms I want but that doesn't make me a leprechaun. Even if it did, new habits take work, not luck.

Mom's been reading up on codependency. Trying to get tough all of a sudden. Hope it helps her cause it's making my life miserable. Not interested in using cocaine but I don't want to follow this pushy legion of rules either. The church counselor says, "You have to follow a guideline to be successful." I'll prove her wrong.

First probation check-in is today. I smoked weed with a friend the other day but I'm prepared. A pill bottle with clean urine, covered in aluminum foil, and held tight in the right spot. One prick of the thumbnail and a yellow stream flows forth as if it's my own. Being a girl is useful. The problem comes when they show up at the house three weeks later, demanding a home screening.

Back to the slammer.

Hate court when I'm home but can't wait to go when I'm here. Pretty self-explanatory. One may get you in, the other could get you out.

We walk from the jailhouse to the courthouse and wait in a tiny holding cell until our names are called. S is the 19th letter of the alphabet so I'm here for the afternoon. It's all good. Nice to be gone from the same four walls. No matter where you go. And the possibility of leniency is enough to make any captive's day.

Most of my time in jail is spent getting my head right. Communicating with God, that is. It's the only thing that satisfies my soul.

I love you, Lord, and I know this is not what You want for me. No matter what happens in court today, I'm going to change. I hate this life. I miss my children. I need Your help. Please, help me.

"Texas Stready, you're up next," the bailiff advises.

Everyone back in the dorm knows how I feel about God. This leaves them expecting something great.

"What happened? What happened?" the girls shout when I return from court.

"Reinstated! Can you believe that? That never happens. Not even with a lawyer. Wow, God is so good."

Mom came to speak at a chapel service last week. I can't believe they let her in. Must not realize she's my mother. I was so happy just to wrap my arms around her. I explain that it was only weed. One bad decision. She knows I'm tired of this life. But can I make it different? Can't help but doubt myself. It never works the way I promise.

I'm as confused as anyone else. The thing that gives me confidence this round is that God looks at the heart. He know's the truth even when I don't, and He's letting me go home. Makes me sure I'll make it this time.

Two months home, then gone again. Falling holds way more excitement than balancing on the tightrope of sobriety.

At Art's Pool Hall one night I meet a wealthy white man by the name of Mike Harrington. He invites a group of us to his house. An exquisite home at the front of a luxury community he developed. There's a full bar. A tray of cocaine and straw is laid out on the bathroom counter. Love this kinda show-off.

After our third date, I sleep with him. "I'm crazy about you, Texas," he declares. "Why don't you move in here? There's nothing I won't do for you."

Great option, so I do. But it's not for me. Too slow. No one can afford to keep me as high as I'm used to being. With the first distraction I'm gone.

Violation number three lands me in a program. First Step. Sixty days later I graduate. I'm always the one they think will make it. Not because I'm a good liar, but because I know what's real and truly want different.

Not too long and I'm back on the streets. Using hard. I'm selective about who sees me in this condition. I've slept with plenty of people and none without cause, but I prefer returning to the old ones. Less work. Or maybe I'm convinced it's less trashy. If I've already done it, it's done. So why not milk 'em for all they're worth.

I hear Billy King has a beautiful home in Golden Gate. I get the address from his sister one night and surprise him. When I arrive, a bunch of people are hanging around his pool. The place is nice. Reminds me of the good old days. Drugs erase the horrors of the past. That, or they sketch a beautiful portrait of the future. Disillusionment. Anything to stay out of today.

I can tell by the look on his face, Billy's happy I'm here. When we're alone in the kitchen he offers to move me in and take care of me. Can't do it. It's a two way street. In one direction I can't trust him but in the other I won't commit.

He started smoking rocks a few years back. Can't believe it though. He never was one to use coke of any kind. "Makes my heart beat too fast," he'd say.

I'm disappointed. He must have quit, otherwise he wouldn't be living like this.

When the party dies out, he pulls a tray from beneath the bar. Guess he does still smoke because he starts rolling a juice-joint (marijuana with crack crumbled inside). That's how he smokes his dope. We smoke hard for a few hours. I use the pipe and he uses weed. Just what I hoped for.

Sleeping with him is automatic but not enjoyed. He robbed me of that possibility years ago. Don't care though. It's what I came here for. I get mine and he gets his. All's fair in love and war. And this life? It's all out war.

Been staying at a girlfriend's house but I need transportation. Can't stay high with no dope and can't keep dope with no hustle. How will I get a vehicle?

Tomas. A nice-looking older Spanish man who's been fantasizing about me since I was seventeen. He's gladly given me thousands of dollars just because. After all this time with no demands, I feel bad. Not a hard choice, it's only right to sleep with the man if he buys me a car.

Saturday morning after a two minute naked roll, he's satisfied. Then we're off to the auction to pick out my new car. A black, Audi-A6, with cream colored leather interior. Nice ride. By Monday I'm tagged, titled, and insured. This takes my game closer to its usual zone. Since I left home in '86 my survival's depended on sales. In Missouri it was Mary Kay. Different product, same dynamics. Introduce people to something that makes them feel better, then be sure to have it available and deliver it on time.

"Gotta keep ya hustle tight," Jo-Jo's tired record still skips through my memory.

One day, on my now rare travels through the projects, I run across my old pal, Shove. He's only been out of prison for a week and already he's back on it. Crack cocaine. He thinks it's a secret but everyone knows. He's the kinda smoker that makes things happen. Never been with a hard-core addict. I figure a relationship can only handle one of those and that's my role.

We hookup. Staying in hotels, hustling dope. Robbing and fooling people. Rebels with the wrong cause. He's a chauvinistic druggie. I don't have to do anything. Just keep up with the drugs and whatnot. If we had a mission statement it would be: Anything for the next hit.

When options run thin he talks me into a title loan. "When I happen along a good come-up, I'll make it right, Tee. You know I will." I'm not used to allowing someone else to make decisions. Especially when it comes to money or drugs. This particular system of drug dependency is new to me. I let him.

Our time together is heedless. Daring. Great fun. Every time I take a hit he says, "Hol' it, Tee. Hol' it long as you can. Good gurl." Such a fun routine.

I get stopped outside our room one night. Cops search the car and find a tiny weed roach—back to the chicken coop.

I've learned to keep what I call a Fallout Plan. Shove and I got so wild I lost track of people. That means there's nobody to pour into my commissary account, come visit, and my car is history. Got to get off this Ferris wheel.

Dizzy.

25

ALONG CAME A SPIDER

Little Miss Muffet,
Sat on a tuffet,
Eating her curds and whey.
Along came a spider,
And set down beside her,
And frightened Miss Muffet away.

A few days in and I'm feeling better. Relieved. Happens faster each arrest. *Sorry Lord. I really do love you. I don't know why I can't do what's right. I honestly don't care what it takes, just make me different. Please, God, I beg you.*

Eleven days later they call my name over the loudspeaker "Pack it up, Stready. You're out. The charges were dropped."

"What? No prison?" I fall to my knees and praise God. He's amazing. Keeps giving me undeserved chances.

Processed and released, but not until midnight. I have no one to pick me up and nowhere to go. Never bothered to call my parents. What would I have said? I stand in front of the jail dizzy with irritation. Troubled.

"Texas, Texas. Look here." I see a dark colored Cadillac in the corner of the parking lot. Someone's waving me over. Without hesitation I head that way. Glad to be seen.

It's Jonas. A dealer I slept with for a few months in the early 90s. Only seventeen and I was twenty-five. His total adoration for me left me spellbound. Happened during one of Bubba and my many splits. I can see in his eyes nothing's changed. I run to him and he picks me up off my feet kissing my face and neck. He's waiting on a tow truck. Flat tire.

"Where ya been, Bae? Man have I missed you. You know you da luv of my life, right, Bae?"

Where do I end up you ask? Same trails, different details. Doesn't look like I'll ever get right, but at least I'm good at wrong.

Can't tell you what lands me back at Wallace's. Probably that his place is always jumpin' and my hookup lives a block over. People come and give their money to him. He brings it in the bedroom. Out the slider and on the moped I go. Down the street and back in a flash. The customer leaves with their product and we smoke-out. Good system. Keeps me from meeting strangers. That's the safest way to do this dirt. No pressure, no problems. I like it.

Wally's sister is a nut job. She didn't stay here when I moved in before, but she's here now. Her bossy, erratic behavior is more than I can deal with. A druggie friend from years back sees me at the Circle K. There's nothing between us, he just knows I know all the right people.

"Hey, Tex. My dad's gone for six months and I have the house to myself. Why don't you come hang with me for a while."

It's a typical Florida home. Everything here is in order and works great. Just a bit outdated is all. Within the week I'm depressed. Nowhere near enough action for me. I'm sober too often. This leaves me with no power to ward off undesired concern. Stuck here. Just me and my demons.

It's close to the projects. Haven't run around in there since my brief time with Shove. Project gossip becomes highly untamed once introduced to the limelight. One trip there and you can get the lowdown on anyone.

Can't go there. I'm ashamed. The people there are like family. As if staying away's enough. Another unrealistic game I play.

I need help. I don't want to live like this. I have a great family who loves me. Three beautiful babies who need me. Can't do this anymore. Been in and out of jails, rehabs, homes. Had prophetic words, prayer vigils and chance after chance.

Is there any such thing as help?

"You need a Christian program, Texas. This is a spiritual problem," my parents say. I get it. Nothing else has worked. Desperate for change I pack up. Mom and Dorothy are my escorts. They drive me across the state to a program named Born Free.

Bottom line? Too radical for me. The director accuses me of performing witchcraft on my family. Really? Swallowed a lot of pills in my day but this is a dose I can't get down. Even with holy water.

"You people are crazy. I will not subject myself to this judgment. My life's bad enough without this so-called help. No frickin' thank you."

"We brought you here to be in this program. We will not take you back," the dynamic duo reports. Mom and Dorothy unload my belongings on the curb, and leave me standing there.

My father's family lives on this coast of Florida. Cocoa Beach. A few phone calls and I get my cousin Robert's cell number. He's had his own issues so there's no judgement. I'm sure he'll let me stay with him for a while. He's 12 years older than me but we've always been close. In a flash he's on his way to rescue me.

Robert owns a gorgeous condominium off the Indian River. Breathtaking. Most days I lay by the pool. Church with Aunt Sallie on Sundays and clearance shopping on Tuesdays. There's nothing better than sale items. We raid the racks at Marshall's and TJ Max. She buys me an outfit each week. Aunt Sallie's always been generous.

Folks told me I needed to leave Naples. Maybe they're right, this change of location does seem to be helping.

Robert gets home about 4 o'clock each afternoon. He loves to cook. He drinks the entire time he's making dinner. Naturally, it's 9 p.m. by the time we eat.

Alcohol keeps me from craving the other stuff. Not only that, if you drink enough you get tired. Hibernation. That's what it feels like. Whatever it is, it's a masterful cure for boredom.

On Friday nights I get dressed in my new outfit and we head to the tiki bar. It's located by the port. That's where the shrimp boats dock. One evening I get antsy at the bar. Without wrongful intent I decide to take a stroll down the boardwalk. Never hung with any shrimpers or fishermen, but one short chat and I see how they roll.

These men spend three months at a time out to sea. When they dock they have a six to eight thousand dollar check. More if he's a captain. First stop's the bank. Then Walmart where they buy supplies. Deodorant, razors, socks, or underwear. The total's two hundred bucks at best.

Guess what they do with the rest? Get high. You got it.

No matter what I do or where I go, drugs show up. It's been a while since these guys have seen a woman or been high; they become pretty much useless in every area except the money-spending department. Easy prey.

I never make it back to the tiki bar. I ring Robert and tell him to go home without me.

On my first travels to the Cocoa crack scene, I meet Jari. They call him, Jay. His parents own the corner store in the black section. Jay's 26 and I'm 33 but I definitely have his un-divided attention. He's a cocaine distributor for a major part of this area. What d'ya know?

Before long I'm smoking like an unkept grill that caught fire. Attached by the stem (crack pipe) to Jay. After a week together I go to Robert's to get my belongings. Then Jay takes me to several stores. "Pick out whatever you need, Texas. I got you, Bae."

When I put my things in the trunk at the condo, I noticed Jay's belongings strewn all over. This makes me decide to get two rolling duffel bags—one red, one blue—with matching cosmetic cases. A bathing suit, sexy night clothes, bath gels, and body lotions. Anything that catches my eye.

He gets a room in a beautiful hotel on the beach. We un-load the contents of the trunk so I can organize both our be-longings. "This will help us move around with ease." I say with a helpful smile. Jay loves this about me.

He also has a motel room. A dive. A place where spenders can use. That's where we are most of the time. The money's what gets him off. He smokes weed but nothing else. The in-coming Benjamins are enough to keep him alert.

I'm a trophy. Good deal. Every time somebody spends another couple hundred, Jay hands me a few pieces. I stash them in my purse and proceed to smoke whatever the person at the table's got. The buyer's don't come on to me because they don't want to make him mad. Months without female interaction and the quality of the product keeps them disoriented. I can do as much of their dope as they do. Love it.

★ ★ ★

He sells to several hustlers in town, as well. Before long I'm the girl that everybody wants to have or be. Extremely valuable. Every few days we go back to our elegant hotel to shower and sleep. I hardly ever do the sleep part. I check my stash. Twenty-eight rocks. Not hard to figure what I do while he's in shutdown mode. Smoke.

Jay wakes. He's hungry. He insists I eat each day. I've gotten quite good at the chew, chew, swallow deal over the years. Don't want to look like some crack-head. If you go too many days without food, you can't get high anyway. That alone's enough to make me eat. When I look back over the years of my life, this is the time when I felt best about my appearance. Thirty-three years old and hot to trot.

Staying awake too long is a disturbing practice. Dangerous. You become unaware. Jay doesn't sleep much either. He's every bit as addicted to money as I am to the rock.

Not a real nice guy. Only takes weeks till the abuse kicks in. No hitting, too scared of jail, but the words he shoots blow through me like a cannon. All his friends are black and he has two black children of his own. Yet I'm the, "d----suckin', n------lovin' b----." Rough wording but that's not even the worst of it.

I get high and act like it doesn't bother me. Most of the time. When I do respond I tend to flip out. Never been the kind of girl to get walked on, but I've learned to calm myself down. It'd be plain old stupid to screw this up.

I say things like, "You love this, don't you? Makes you feel like a man. You don't affect me. Can I get another hit or what?"

I phone my kids whenever we go to our own room. Just to remind them who I am. I miss them terribly but I'm in no condition to be their mother. It's better this way. At least that's what I tell myself.

I talked to Mom yesterday. She invited me to come for a birthday party. I'm gonna ask Jay about going. Don't want to miss Jordan and my birthday celebration. Over the years I've done my best to be there for all of my children's birthdays or holidays. Mom always does something for them. Where would they be without her, or their dad for that matter?

Don't speak of it often. Ignoring this pain has become a way of life. Still all it takes is a sight or a sound to revive the self-hatred I have for not loving them properly. Ashamed.

No matter how long I stay straight or what good I accomplish the voice of wasted time obsesses over their undeserved treatment. Overwhelming regret has pushed me back to drugs on countless occasions.

Jay shakes me till my eyes open. Fell asleep crying. The crack stem dropped to my lap, scorched through my jeans, and into my thigh. The burn is bad. I'd been up for five days so the pain didn't even wake me. Wish it had burst into flames. Then all this shit would be over. Don't have the balls to kill myself but dead's gotta be better than wandering through this point-less maze.

I take a hit and head for the shower. Next comes I-HOP. Haven't been home in five months. Over breakfast I tell him about the conversation with my mother. "Please, baby. Please take me. You'll love my family. Everyone does."

My people are kind and fair. Still I wonder what they'll think of this one.

Nervous.

26

ONE SHOE ON

Diddle, diddle, dumpling, my son John,
Went to bed with one shoe on;
One shoe off, and the other shoe on,
Diddle, diddle, dumpling, my son John.

The ride to Naples is rough. Old boyfriends the topic. Raw and uncomfortable, like an open blister. No cocaine going into me and no money coming in for him. We're both jonesin'. No dope, combined with the thought of seeing my kids, is more than my head can handle.

Last week Jay had his parents purchase him a brand-new, royal blue, Lincoln LS—his money, of course. If emotions were mud, the white leather interior would be filthy. Tears and fears smeared everywhere. His brutal accusations and insecure name-calling is sharp and spiteful.

When madness settles, Jay tells me he wants out of this lifestyle. "I've saved $189,000, Texas. If you'll stop using, I'll stop selling, and we'll move to Bradenton, Florida. You with that?" I agree. Partly because I know I can't stay this high without him and partly because faith reminds me there's a better way.

Our trip to Naples is wonderful. Everyone's pleasant to Jay. So good to see my family. I have outfits for all three of my children and special birthday gifts for Jordan. Why can't it be like this every day?

★ ★ ★

Nervous about this move. Can't believe I'm doing it. We'll be living with his parents and his younger brother, Hamza. They are Muslims, but only his mom practices the traditions. Although the responsibility doesn't sit well with me, I realize my example of Christ isn't a very good one.

His mother and I become friends. One day, as she makes fresh hummus and I do the dishes, Fatima sneezes. Years ago I heard a story about the reason people use the phrase, "God bless you." Didn't agree, so I stopped using it.

"Why is it you never bless me when I sneeze?" she asks.

Throughout my life I have remained aware of God's voice. In this moment I hear His Spirit tell me, "She's right you know. You should take every opportunity available to bless people."

"I'm so sorry, Fatima. You're right. May God bless you."

She smiles and goes back to work. The entire time I'm here, I do everything I can to be loving and gentle. That's how God has treated me.

We move into our own place. Nice to decorate and take care of a home. Haven't done that in years. But I'm settling. I'd rather have a free place to live, trips to Naples with a car full of gifts, and a guaranteed way to get my needs met. Don't have what it takes to go for change again. If I don't make it I'll be in big trouble.

When you become accustomed to using a certain amount of drugs, never again are you able to enjoy the former status quo. Harsh truth to identify. With Jay, my supply was enormous and constant. It's not probable I'll find a way to match that. I'm not a young plum. Matter of fact, getting closer and closer to prune status. Better stay right here.

Like most Middle Eastern entrepreneurs, Jay's good at generating the almighty dollar. Computer components is his new enterprise. The business keeps him from dipping into his savings. He's cool with that at first but like every addiction, desire goes from a suggestion to a demand. He's always at work. I'm lonely, but safe from myself and my toxic habits. I must *make* this be enough.

He's an angry and controlling man. Boy, really. If he calls me one more name this week, I think I'll slash his tires. Real mature. The cons are beating the pros, and I'm not talking criminals or football.

Verbal abuse is vicious. He spent most of his time in the hood but every other sentence is filled with hatred for who I've loved and why. Some of his words are true, making my existence thorny and tiresome. More like a four year trick than a relationship.

At least prostitutes get their money and go about their business. I'm stranded here. Living a lie. Cooking, cleaning, and faking orgasms. Without intoxicants my shiny justifications are losing their luster. Quickly.

The phone wakes me. It's my brother's wife, Nicole. "Turn on the TV. Turn on the TV. An airplane just flew into the World Trade Center."

I push POWER on the remote just in time to watch the second plane crash into the building. Everyone remembers where they were when they heard this news. Me? I was asleep in the bed of an Arab Muslim. Wouldn't you know it?

I attempt to maintain stability by venting to my mom. Not intimidated by him physically or politically. Cruel enough to myself, that's all. Tired of empty.

Mom encourages I leave, "This is not God's best for you, Texas. It can't be. He has so much better for you, baby. Come home." My soul repeats her words. "You're only one decision away from a new direction."

Jay's brother, Hamza, drops by to smoke weed with me. Often. On occasion he brings a friend or two. Today it's a girl from his high school days. Kelly. She begins to stop by every couple of days. Gives me rides to appointments or the grocery store. One day we decide to go to Ross. It's right down the road and of course they have clearance racks.

A regular priced shirt that has no security tag starts the downward spiral. Before long we're using wire cutters to remove sensors and walking from the store; carts full of un-purchased clothing. Months of weekly trips and ridiculous antics find us held up in a Manatee County squad car. Booked and jailed.

I call Jay but he hangs up on me. Furious. In 24-hour court the next morning, I'm released on my own recognizance. They always give you one shot and I've never been arrested here.

Desperate disgust burns in my bones like battery acid on an old paint job. What was I thinking and how do I go home to this man? Why would I?

No choice, that's why. Like an overused jacket ragged and worn, this relationship has become nothing more than an un-attractive habit.

Homecoming's not a happy event. After Jay calms down and calls it a night I stay up downloading music from Kazaa. "You're only one decision away from a new direction." I hear Mom's plea.

His breath is heavy and the wood floor creeks as I discreetly inch into the room. From beneath the bed I pull my bag and stuff it fat with belongings. Then down the street I stroll. Just me, my shadow, and my rolling duffle bag. I catch a ride to I-75. A trucker then picks me up and escorts me all the way to the Golden Gate exit. Naples.

A jigsaw puzzle with no picture. I keep trying to connect life's pieces. Thought sure Master Jo-Jo had all the answers. No doubt his intentions were perverted—still God wastes nothing. Prayers from friends around the globe activated spiritual interference. In many instances He used those twisted rules to save my life.

Confusing to know the truth so well but still buy into the lies. I wonder if the accident really did mess up my head. Something's gotta be wrong with me. What's it gonna take? Hitting bottom means nothing. I've fallen through the bottom—more than once.

Embarrassment from my recent arrest keeps me from calling my folks. Been off cocaine for two years but walking down the street in Naples turns the old crave on. Full blast.

I've always been lucky. Won $1,500 first time at the dog track and $350 at the Daytona 500. So imagine who I run into at the first gas station? Mike Harrington. The wealthy white man who owns the big house. The one I left pouting in the dust. Couldn't have paid for a better scenario.

I'm uneasy. What if he hates me? Chill girl, your mindset determines what you end up with and you know this. I leave my bag outside and walk in. Took $60 out of Jay's wallet and $14 from the truckers backpack. At the counter I order a pack of Newport shorts. Mike notices me, and as if cornered by a hypnotic flashback he stares and says, "Texas, is that you?"

"Mike. How are you?"

"I'm great and you?"

"Seen better days that's for certain. But you know me, I'll make it."

"Let Mikey take you for coffee," he suggests. "You can tell me all about it." We walk from the store.

"Where's your car?" he asks.

"Not here," is all I say. I close the door to his silver Cadillac and point to the front of the store. "Will you pull up there and get my bag?" Wearing a shocked expression, he drives over, jumps out, and tosses the bag into the trunk.

"Texas, are you okay?" I rub my face and shake my head.

"Don't be embarrassed. It doesn't matter to me what's going on, sweetheart. You're good now." He reaches over and pats my back like I'm some child who fell on the playground.

After breakfast I gladly consent to stay in his well-equipped, immaculate home; thrilled to do as much of his cocaine as I can get up my nose.

Weeks pass and snorting becomes impossible. My sinuses can't stand it. One day while he's at a meeting I turn on the stove top, grab a spoon, and some baking soda. Within minutes, crack it is.

Don't own a stem so I have to do it the old-school way. I grab a Minute Maid can from the garbage, light three cigarettes for ashes, and with the tack that holds the kitchen calendar, I carefully craft a pipe. Ingenious.

Mike snorts on occasion but he's not much into the co-caine scene. He'd never smoke. Females are his drug of choice. He keeps cocaine around because, like my boyfriend Sean use to say, "Girls on cocaine are capable of anything." Thank god he's not into freaky stuff. Not that I know of. Don't get down like that.

I'm in the kitchen when the door lock turns. Mike walks in and I can tell by his expression he smells the smoke. He's not bothered, just happy I'm still here. Cool.

I have court on the 23rd of the month. Thank goodness for Mike. Not only will he get me to court, I'll have commissary money too. I'm gonna do time. Too much of a record to walk with probation. It's almost like I win either way—God is there to salvage me from disaster, or the enemy hangs out making sure my fall from grace has some cushion. Promise or poison. A nonstop tug-of-war.

One hundred and twenty days in the Manatee County Jail. That's my sentence. It's the most time I've done. At least it's nice here. Lots of classes and programs. And Mike sends money each week. Way better than my hometown jail.

I call Mom from jail. She's surprised by my charges but happy I'm away from Jay. She's learned not to ask questions she doesn't want answers to. Lying's overrated. She tells me to call her once every other week.

Been gone from Naples for three years. Dad's the foremen for a big deal builder in Marco Island and Mom's the associate pastor at a new church. The best salary she's ever had. These two factors in addition to their inheritance money allow them to begin building their dream home.

"The house is unbelievable, Texas." Mom tells when I call. "Can't wait for you to see it. I'll send pictures."

"Don't you dare. I want to be totally surprised, Catwoman." We laugh and hang up.

My release date comes and after a weekend in a penthouse suite in Sarasota Beach, Mike takes me to see my parents. McCauley Culkin in Home Alone—that's what I look like. Both hands on both cheeks and mouth in an open oval; all I can do is scream. When I turn each corner I do it again.

"Oh my gosh! Oh my gosh! This is our house? *Our* house? Oh my gosh! It's beautiful. So beautiful."

My parents have had it hard. They deserve this. Their life seems like they're trying to run an uphill race with one leg. I guess it's like that for everyone at times.

Hopping.

27

WHEN SHE COMES

She'll be coming around the mountain when she comes
She'll be coming around the mountain when she comes
She'll be coming around the mountain,
She'll be coming around the mountain,
She'll be coming around the mountain,
When she comes.

Ditched Mike. No need for him. Gonna do it right this time. I'm privileged to have my own beautiful bedroom and bathroom in my parent's gorgeous home. My ex-husband Bubba is the maintenance man at the same apartment complex he moved to when we separated. It happens to be catty-corner from the new house. For the last three years, I've talked to my children at least twice a week and seen them as often as possible. But for the first time in forever they have direct access to me. So happy.

While I was locked-up in St. Pete, they put me on medication. Psych meds and non-narcotic pain relievers. I have herniated discs in my back, ones that bulge in my neck, a bad knee and forearm. The accident. Amazingly enough, my pain is minimal.

It doesn't take much to tell. Been dabbling again since I've been home. And my shoulder wears more than one chip. Not on purpose. Exasperated expressions on family faces feel cold.

Guilt. Been at this for two decades. My well-smoked pipe-dreams seem ridiculous. Even to me. I can hardly stand myself. As much as I long for freedom, entrapment is good at finding a way to stare me down and cripple me.

Reasons are heavy and I'm in no shape to be lugging them around. Still everybody expects one. I took the medication in jail just cause I could. Not like I had a better option. Who knows, maybe I am halfway crazy.

Today's my first appointment. Dr. Fawcett. Got his name from a dude at an NA meeting. I figure if you have to go to the doctor it should be the kind that prescribes the good stuff, and meeting goers always know who addicts should stay away from.

Hopping into his office as if I'm in tremendous pain, I leave with a handful of scripts. Happy-happy, joy-joy. Forgot how fun legal drugs are. No cost, no crime. Can't beat that.

With a full bottle in hand, who can take just one. It's like drinking decaffeinated coffee. Pointless. Three, turns to five, then eight. Can't remember how many I've downed today or when I took them last.

Twenty years have passed since my first toke of weed. A long time. Captured by shame and resentment, I felt certain high was my only way out. I remember the first time Dad kidnapped me from Jo-Jo Jackson's. The next afternoon, in a humble attempt to fill our rotting relationship, Mom told me this story.

"When I was eighteen your father joined the Army. He was stationed in Germany. My sister Cheree had only died three years earlier and your grandparents were still heartbroken. I took on the responsibility of keeping my parents happy. It was a terrible burden to carry. With my boyfriend gone, I felt all alone. I decided to take a trip and spend the summer with my mother's family in Rhode Island.

"People there were different from my circle of friends. Instead of going to youth group they went to bars. Desperate for company, I went too. One evening after a few drinks I went home with a boy named Butch. I became pregnant that evening.

"When I came home I told only two friends. Although my conscience wouldn't allow me to tell my parents, I could not keep it from your dad.

"He offered to keep the baby and claim it as his own, but I couldn't do that. I knew he was going to seminary and that people would say, 'The baby looks just like you, Bob,' and things of that nature. Our life would be a lie.

"We got married and moved to California where I gave birth to my first child. A daughter.

"I'm telling you this because I want you to understand I haven't done everything right in my life either. I'm sorry that things have been so difficult for you. I want you to know that I love you and I don't expect you to be perfect."

My reaction was lifeless. I stared at the wall until she left the room. I ran away as a teenager from a life I considered fake. Nothing could alter my view. At thirty-seven, I still wouldn't call myself happy about the sister deal, but I'm past that other stuff and I'm dying to know who she is.

Mom makes contact and one Thursday a month later our sister's on a plane. My take on life's not what you'd define as rational. How will I properly evaluate and enter into this new union? The thought is strange. Surreal.

The evening arrives and the family gathers. I can tell my mother's anxious and excited. Can't help but feel happy for her.

What a huge void she must've had all these years. Maybe that's part of our disconnect. This could be the very thing that makes us better.

Dorene Stier. Dori, that's her name. With noisemakers, streamers and signs that read, "Finding Dori," we wait in the Delta terminal eager to meet our missing sibling.

Awesome week. I stay pretty much sober. My pills are too scarce to enjoy. Just enough to get me through.

Dori's gentle and sincere. No judgment or anger. By the time she leaves we're all joking and pulling pranks. She fits right in. As if I had a big sister all the while. Relieved.

There's work to be done. I need an SSI check. I was taken care of when I had a man so I wasn't willing to fill out the forms and visit the doctors required to get cash. Medicaid was immediate and that covered doctor's visits and medication. The world better look out—all I need is one more green light before I'll be collecting a free pay check. Sweet.

With illegal activity gone from my life things are much more manageable. Funny thing, I won't take pills for depression—they're hard on your liver and I have hepatitis C—but I'll chew five Percocet 10s four times a day. Absurd. I've learned to ration them out. I'd like to take ten, three times a day but if I do they're gone way too fast.

Next weekend my sister-in-law Dorothy and some friends are going to Lake Placid. The house there has been in my family since I was born. My mother's folks built it as a retirement home when they lived in Miami. Now that they're gone it belongs to my parents. I can tell Dorothy's hesitant to take me. The pills, I'm sure. Not wanting me to feel left out she asks,

"You interested in going to the lake with me and the girls this weekend?"

"I'd love to."

"Okay, but no drugs, Texas. Got it?"

"Okay, okay, no prob," I say without hesitation.

I'm low on pills. Seems no matter how many I have I'm always saying that. But this time I am low. Only ten left. That means I won't be able to be high this weekend anyway. Time away from here. Just what the doctor ordered.

I haven't been to the lake in years. The dock's collapsing. Got pretty trashed in the last hurricane. In case you don't know this, people on pills can do anything, let them tell it. Convinced it would be no big deal to walk out on the dock, I go for it. Two steps and a dry-rotted board gives way. My ankle twists and I fall through.

With only eight pills left and a powerful tolerance, I'm in terrible pain. I end up taking them all within the next three hours. By midnight Dorothy's forced to take me to the ER. It's in Sebring, thirty minutes out. She's pissed.

She drops me off and drives away. Doesn't return until she's leaving for home—fifteen hours later. My ankle is demolished. Broken in three places and needs replacing. Only a specialist can repair it. I'm not upset. Great excuse. Now I can get the Doc to bump up the quality and quantity of my prescriptions.

When I get home, Mom takes me to a surgeon to see about getting the work done. The doctor I see doesn't take Medicaid. He explains to me how delicate these bones are. The repair's a fragile job. Tedious. In a tone somewhere between sad and solvent I vow to pay in small but faithful increments.

"Please sir? You can't leave me like this." He smiles and calls in the scheduling nurse.

★ ★ ★

We're the best of friends now, but at this point in the story my ex-husband and I can't stand each other. We argue and fight when we're in the same room. I'm still angry and hurt. Why wouldn't he just do the work to correct our marriage?

"You should be giving Justice his medicine at the exact same time every day." I say. "He's regressing. Thirteen and hasn't said anything for years. At least when I was around he talked some."

I was a thorough and attentive mom. Now my poor children don't have me. Disgrace. Guess that's why I pick fights.

I often walk across the street to his apartment to see my kids. Not usually a drinker but this evening I tip a few tall ones. Too few pills to create a smile and too much shame to mask. I can fix that. Alcohol's good at amping up the hydro effect. Hydrocodone, that is.

Bubba's been sober since before Justice was born. But like any good alcoholic he can still smell booze the moment it cracks the door.

"You been drinkin'? Don't be comin' here drunk, Texas."

"Shut up, Bubba. You can't keep me from seeing my children. You're the most unhappy person I've ever known. You'd find something wrong with Jesus Christ." He puts his hand on my chest and pushes me back trying to close the door.

"Take your hands off me. You're not my husband anymore. Thank god."

His neighbors hear the commotion and call the police. An officer rolls up. Inches from Bubba's face I call him every name I can think of. Alcohol drowns intelligence. Without doubt.

The officer says, "Just tell me you'll press charges and I'll take her away."

"Naw, I'm not pressin' charges. Dat's the alcohol talkin'. Jus leave, Texas."

"You can't make me leave. Where are my damn kids?"

The officer grabs my arm to move me and I pull away from him. "That's resisting arrest, young lady."

"I'm not under arrest. For what?" I ask pulling my arm from him again.

"Now it's resisting with violence."

"You're stupid. Let me go."

"That's battery on a LEO." He forcefully takes control of me. "You have the right to remain silent…"

Collier County Jail. Been a little minute since I've been here. The building's in the process of an upgrade but, believe it or not, most of the officers and inmates are the same. This county loves to keep you jailed. I heard the state pays them $54 a day, per inmate. If that's true the new building's sure to be the most modern rattrap available.

The charge sticks. Battery on a Law Enforcement Officer. Insane. It carries an enormous number of points. Excessive even. My record's already packed with them. Points determine whether you go to prison or not, and for how long.

My public defender tells me there's nothing I can do to combat this charge. His word against mine. Sheriff versus felon. Never a fair fight.

After sixty-eight days, I consent to a plea agreement. No contest, for a year and a day in the Florida Department of Corrections. I'm okay with it—kinda. Everyone swears it's better than jail but I'd be lying if I said the thought doesn't shake me.

It won't be that big a deal. That's what I tell myself. They gave me an additional forty-five days credit for time I served who knows when. No complaints. I'll have another month in by the time I make it to the compound. In Florida you do 85% of your sentence—ten months on a year. Leaves me with about five months to the finish line.

And so I sit. Anxiously awaiting this new form of slavery. Can't believe it's finally come to this.

Wow.

28

BLACK SHEEP

Baa, baa, black sheep,
Have you any wool?
Yes, sir, yes, sir,
Three bags full;
One for the master,
And one for the dame,
And one for the little boy
Who lives down the lane.

It's the worst. R-n-O. Rules and Orientation. Over one hundred girls in an open space, a pushy officer stationed right there with you. We each have a single bed and a plastic bin to hold our belongings. Throughout the day our area is subject to search. Things must be in perfect order—beds without wrinkle, clothes without crease—from 3:30 a.m. till 8:30 p.m. Like bootcamp, minus the honor.

At 4:00 a.m., 10:30 a.m., and 4:00 p.m., we're to be in dual lines ready to walk to the chow hall. Other than your section's ten minute shower time and an occasional sympathy break, there is no talking.

Between meals we sit on the edge of our bed. If you're caught whispering or dozing, you're forced to stand at the foot of your bed. All day, everyday, is spent in an upright position listening to an officer recite the guidelines for institutional living. This way, when you break a rule, there's no such thing as "I didn't know…"

The best part is definitely the walk to meals. We're outdoors—wow. There's a huge fence around the place but if you don't look that far you can ignore it. There's grass, trees, bugs, ducks and lizards. Notice them all, first trip. After three months in jail it's nice to see any form of nature.

When we arrive at the dining annex, we stand in line until the group ahead of us leaves. Looks like a school cafeteria. Once seated, you have 15 minutes to eat, dump your tray and get back in line. No questions, no comments. The experience brings distinct clarity to the term "fast-food."

After two and a half weeks of this painful process I'm teamed out to regular housing. I'm a short-timer so they don't want to spend money sending me to a different facility. Cool with that. It's only a few hours from Naples and I'm sure my parents will come visit me. At least once.

I'm in A-Dorm. After two weeks I learn my way around. Looks similar to jail but at least you have some kinda life here. You can walk to the field on the weekends and sit on the bleachers. You order things in the canteen line and receive them right then. You have a job and go to it five days a week.

One evening a team of COs rush into the dorm blowing whistles and shouting, "Hit the floor, ladies. Facedown on the floor."

People are grumbling, "Carol got caught with dope. If they don't find where it came from they'll shut this unit down. We'll all have to move."

After being sprawled-out on the floor for over an hour they begin to instruct us to stand, four at a time. "Pack your belongings, sheets, and towels—then lineup."

The five best inmates in this unit are moved to D-Dorm. "Damnation Dorm," the lifer block. I just so happen to be one of the fantastic five. I suppose it makes sense but it doesn't seem fair. The girls they keep here don't even have jobs. Too dangerous. Most are mental and that's putting it nicely. Don't care about following the rules cause they got nothin' but time. Hopeless.

My bunky seems cool. They call her Susie Q. She's in for murder. A robbery gone sour. Don't remember the details, only that more than one person died. Wonder if these people were loco before? Or did the life sentence do it? Most of them are quiet, but a deep and disturbed anger is evident.

I'm only here for a week but that's long enough to hear about Francis Cox. Francis murdered her infant. Cut the baby up and microwaved her. When her husband arrived home she tried to serve him the child for dinner. The reason? Because she found out he had an outside baby on the way. Guess she snapped. Come on, her mind had to be pretty bent to start with.

Then there's Zorro the Hitchhiker. Don't know her real name. They call her that because of her charges. She had the habit of hitchhiking up and down I-75. Only rode with men and only killed the ones that came on to her. Got caught because one of the men lived. A stab wound to the chest and repeated slices all over his body. A hunter found him crawling down a dirt road, twenty-three miles from city limits. After her conviction she told them where to find two other victims. She has sixty-five years, plus two life sentences. "Nothin' but time."

I hear the stories. See the expressions. But I don't waste time trying to understand. Not anymore. It's crazy. At least three times a day I find myself considering what sorta anguish a person must live through to be capable of this or that. Everyone's got a story.

Believe me when I tell you I could fill a book with tragic tales. People are quick to tell you about their own crimes as well as someone else's. And if they think you care at all, they'll accidentally share the crimes perpetrated against them. Horrible, unmentionable things. Stuff that make my complaints appear as David did to Goliath. Insignificant.

Finally restored to my old dorm; relieved to be among the partially sane. My job is inside grounds. It's hot working outside in the Florida sun. Especially in long pants and boots, but I'm grateful to be able to enjoy the open sky. Glad to keep busy.

Never would've considered myself a writer but as I look back over the years of my life, I was always writing. When I wasn't using. In the evening instead of watching TV, doing hair, or playing cards. I spend my time jotting things down. Letters, plans, or thoughts.

Writing keeps my mind focused on what's really happening. It helps me hear God's voice and identify needed changes. Sometimes it takes a while to recognize the obvious. The reason my life is such a mess is because I don't love the Lord enough. That's what I figure.

I begin to ask the Lord about this and He reminds me of the scripture that says, "You have not because you ask not." Honestly it seems a little harsh. I've asked, and asked, and asked. I want things to be different and I don't get why God doesn't just do it. I know He's capable.

The Holy Spirit responds. "You ask Me to *make* you different but I won't *make* you do anything. Ask Me to show you how to *want* different."

I pull out a fresh yellow legal pad and on the top of the first page I write, "Help Me Love You More." That's what I need. I continue to write. "Give me more love for You. Become the most important thing to me. Make me wild about You. Give me a willingness to do anything for You. Show me how to be closer to You."

Before bed each night I think of twenty different ways to say the exact same thing. If asking is what gets results, then I'll ask until God answers.

By the time I'm released my thoughts have changed. Instead of going home to my parents' house I go to the homeless shelter. I want to keep myself accountable. Humility.

St. Matthews House. Here they breathalyze you each evening and give random drug screens. You must be gone from the facility from 9 a.m. to 2 p.m. You also have a daily chore and must attend at least five AA or religious meetings a week.

I love it here. Pleased to be doing it apart from my family. The first thing I do is make myself a schedule. I'm diligent to stay inside the lines. I talk and pray with friends and counselors. Share thoughts and feelings in groups. Structured environments. I do well with them. Institutionalized? Could be. But at least this is a place of my own choosing. I've attempted to plant crops of change in all kinds of soil but choice is the only ground that change can sprout from.

No guy/girl relationships are permitted. Not among clients. There's a guy named William Ferreira. Bill. I'm interested. The forced separation permits us to get to know each other on a deeper level. He's been sober for nine months. Alcohol was his thing. He's part Portuguese and moved here from the city. Boston. Who knows how he landed in Naples but man am I glad he did.

First white boyfriend since high school. Bill is a kind and gentle man. He loves me with the same intensity as the old crowd and I can tell he's honored to have my eye. Feels good. Like a long-lost dream come to life.

I'm approved for Vocational Rehabilitation. I meet with my guidance counselor and together we decide that I should join the cosmetology program at the local vo-tech. My classes and supplies are totally paid for. What a brilliant opportunity God is offering me.

I have passion. Can't remember the last time my life had that. Not just for a man but for a career. A future. Things couldn't be better.

Bill leaves St. Matthew's and moves into a house that rents rooms. Now we can be an actual couple. He's a welder and has an excellent position with a local company. He also leads the Saturday morning AA meeting at The Breakfast Club.

Beauty school will be starting in a month. I'm nervous about the inconvenience of living here. I'll have to leave the shelter early and do five meetings a week, in addition to all day at school. Yuck. I can't afford to eat in the school cafeteria and am unable to keep the materials here to make my own lunch. How will I make this work?

After three weeks of watching my struggle, Bill invites me to move in with him. His room is huge. A renovated garage. It's the best time of my life. I'm happy to wake up and go to school, happy to come home to a man who loves me.

My family relationships are great—everybody loves Bill—including my children. The two of us attend church and meetings regularly. Dad even loans us the money to buy a used Volvo from a dear friend. The nicest car I've ever owned.

This afternoon I'm teaching Jordan to drive. Azlynn's a cheerleader and we're taking Justice to one of her games. Hoo-Hoo still doesn't talk but he loves going places. It's been eight months since prison. Time sure flies on this side of the wall. Real life's become full.

Bill's acting strange tonight. Suspicious. Wonder what's wrong? He takes me to dinner where we had our first date. Alice Sweetwater's. After dinner he takes out a box, grabs my hand and gets down on his knee. "Will you do me the honor of spending the rest of your life with me?"

Through tears of amazement I shout. "Yes! Yes!" The whole restaurant cheers. A wonderful man, beautiful car, lovely home. My education, family relations, and self-worth are chart-busting. For the first time ever, life's a fairytale. Not like anything I'm used to.

Strange.

29

HOW I WONDER

Twinkle, twinkle, little star,
How I wonder what you are!
Up above the world so high,
Like a diamond in the sky.
Twinkle, twinkle, little star,
How I wonder what you are!

My mother's a speaker, teacher, and writer. For years she's encouraged me to share my struggle. "Giving back is important, Texas. It's how you gain purpose."

I've spoken at conferences and meetings on occasion, telling of my hardships and what I believed possible. This time's different. My life is finally beginning to reap the rewards of self-discipline.

My youngest brother, Jed, lives in Melbourne, Florida. He is close friends with the pastor of Promiseland Church. That's how my mother met the pastor's wife. When I was in prison, Mom and Dad went there to visit the church. Mom shared with the two of them all God was accomplishing through this phase of my journey. They were excited.

"When Texas comes home, would the two of you like to come here to do a women's retreat?"

"We'd love to," Mom says.

That tentative appointment is happening this weekend. Can't believe I'm in a place where God can use my mess to help someone else. Strange privilege.

Azlynn and Bill are coming too. A year before my unfortunate trip up the road (prison), Azzie asked me to sign my permission for her to get a tattoo.

"Daddy won't do it, Mom. Will you?"

Knowing she wouldn't agree, I said "Sure, Azlynn, if you'll get the same one as me."

While incarcerated I doodled, considered, and prayed until I came up with a design I thought we'd both agree on. That's part of the reason she's coming this weekend. My brother's enchanted with body ink—big time. He knows an excellent artist. The dude that does his work. If you're going to be marked for life it should be done by an expert. Wouldn't you agree?

Whisper. That's the tattoo. Written in swirling cursive. The line that drops down from the P will circle back and capture the word His. His—God—get it? It will be written behind our right ear as a reminder. Life is full of voices. The world shouts it's opinion in one ear while the Lord's suggestions are still and small. A whisper. There's a butterfly that dots the I, representing the transformation that takes place in your life when you listen to the right whisper. His whisper.

We both love how they turn out. So cool. Proud to sport the same one as my girl.

The conference is awesome. Life's different from what I expected. I think of using quite often but the fun hardly competes with the trouble. Too much junk to deal with. Busy working on positive things. Don't want to let myself or anyone else down. Doesn't matter if I feel like getting high; I'm not doing it.

Twenty-five pounds overweight. Like every bride-to-be I want to look perfect on the big day. Flawless. I have ten months to get that way. I join the gym and due to a trainer's advice I begin taking Hydroxy Cut. I've lost about 4 pounds. Feels kinda good to work up a sweat.

I wake up in the middle of the night and Bill is about four inches from my face. He keeps saying, "You're okay, you're okay." My thinking is stifled, absent somehow. Confused. Wouldn't know what to say if I did speak.

"You had a seizure, baby," Bill reports.

I sit up, but it doesn't help. Facts make no sense.

"It's okay, Texas. You're okay. Just lay back down." Bill holds me close till I fall back to sleep.

Did I tell you my mother knows everything? She does. So in the morning—after Bill explains what happened—the first thing I do is call Mom. She goes right to work, along with the rest of the private investigators in my family.

After days of phone calls, questions, and research we come to the conclusion that the seizure was caused by one of two things. The accident or the Hydroxy Cut. The warning label does prohibit use if you have a seizure condition. Maybe the condition was caused by the accident and the fat-burner activated it. The whole ordeal's unsettling.

After a few months fear fades. The doctor tells me not to take the pills again and that it's probably a one time event. Phew!

I'm so excited. My sister Dori's son, Bryan, is graduating from high school. Mom, Dad, Buddy, Dorothy and I are flying to California. The furthest I've ever traveled. I'll meet my niece and nephews, see Dori's home, and meet her friends.

Can't believe I actually have a sister. I'm in a good place and have so much to be happy about. *Thank you, Lord, for all You're doing.*

We land in San José, California. My sister's hometown is an hour away—Ben Lomond. She's been in the same house since she was born. Mom's prayers have taken good care of her too.

Once we settle in, I call Bill. Something sounds different in his voice. Is he slurring? "Why do you sound like that, Bill?" He hides from my questions but I see the truth. "You've been drinking, haven't you?" I'm instantaneously torn from adventure to alarm. As if I pulled the ripcord to discover no parachute.

Later that evening, I'm caught off guard by the notion to smoke some weed. Too many feelings to deal with. All the meetings I go to tell me better, still my brain convinces me it's okay. Weed's never been the problem. No big deal. I can handle it.

No drug is ever a good idea for an addict. Still I smoke.

I call Bill a few times the next day but he doesn't answer. Sickened by the thoughts but I do my best to ignore my feelings and enjoy my family time. I drink a few glasses of wine at a picnic the next afternoon. I can see concern on my parents' faces but they don't dare say anything. Don't want to set me off.

When I arrive home, Bill's drunk. Sloppy, can't-hold-your-head-up, look-like-an-idiot drunk. I pack a bag and leave. Can't tolerate this.

How can this be true? My hands are tied and my dream's been trampled. Not again. I cry until my chest hurts but the truth's still true. Whether I believe it or not.

I hold on as long as I can. Even move back in a few times. Before this, I never realized the severity of his problem. He's the kind of lush that keeps a bottle under the bed so he can take a sip if he happens to wake up. One thing I've learned the hard way is you don't just snap to and see clearly. Not when the fog's this heavy. He's in too deep. Way too deep.

Wagons don't have seat-belts and Bill seems to get bumped off at every turn. Something in me is devastated but the part of me that understands addiction will barely allow tears. It's not personal. He's lost control.

I rent a room from the friend who sold me the Volvo. A gnarly ball of destruction is rolling straight for me. I dodge it long enough to finish school but not without a slip or two.

I find a job in a high-end salon. By the end of the first week I notice something. I have no idea what I'm doing. Not only that, cosmetology's rough on your back and neck. How come when I was choosing my career the counselor never thought to mention this?

Everything is falling apart. No husband, no job, no place of my own. Been on the much-too-straight and far-too-narrow for better than a year. Sheer willpower. That's how I keep it together. Feels pointless. Who wants to fight and fight a battle you'll never win.

Not I, says the addict…

Been using for three weeks. Quite sure my roommate knows. She has to, my schedule's been crazy. I hooked up with some Naples Park people. Safe place to get dope. Tonight I took a few pills of who knows what when the supply ran out. It's almost 2 a.m.. Gotta head home. I jump in my car and inch from the driveway riding the brake. Shouldn't be behind the wheel.

Don't remember the trip towards home, only that I don't arrive. I rear-end a lady at a red light. Bad news. Worse than that, I don't even stop. Never have been the hit-and-run type no matter what it was I was hitting. Not till tonight. Proving true a sentence I've worn thin—you can run but you can't hide.

The police officer catches me down the street parked in a dark driveway.

Why would I resort to drugs? Each return multiplies the complexity of lies that bind me. Like an infected cell the sickness spreads. There's no such thing as a topical treatment to cure a full body infection and my viral load is through the roof. Ninety days in the CCJ. That's the judge's prescription for my diseased state.

Released. Back at St. Matt's. Safe and secure with renewed determination. Starving pride will feed off anything. Rising to star status is not too tough at the homeless shelter.

I meet this guy by the name of Fletch. Humans are prone to rule-breaking. I've witnessed people jump through a variety of crude hoops attempting to avoid bad feelings. You'd think I'd learned my lesson from my last relationship. Instead here I go jumping again.

We spend our days together and act as if we don't know each other when we're back at the home. The distraction of a relationship is a gentle pacifier. Could it be the comfort of common ground or maybe it's the old desire for mental escape? I don't know.

No one in the family's too terribly impressed with Fletch but at least they don't hate him. He's five years younger than me. Kept his habit under control for many years. Married his high school sweetheart. Kind of a goody-goody, white-boy. Prominent job, extensive travels, and a huge expense account transform him from a mortal to a vampire. Now he has no wife, no job and no life. Addiction. Never a happy ending.

Don't know how but my family still believes. It's downright sad. They've traded hurt and discouraged for helpless and dumbfounded. No clue what love is, how to live right, or what I can trust. The only thing I'm sure of is forgiveness. Experienced it too much not to believe.

Azlynn's at the eight month mark. Pregnant. I was fortunate enough to be living at my mom's when the scare came. We took the test together. Now that the time has come, grace allows me here once more. Happy to be around, if for no other reason, cause she needs me. We see each other regularly and talk daily. I know she doesn't have much respect for me but having a baby makes you want your mama.

In three weeks I'll be a grandmother. Grandma? I never want to be called that. Research informs me that Nona is the Italian name for grandmother. My mother's mother was 100% Italian. It's in the blood. Nona it is.

Only one person can be present when the baby's born. The baby's daddy says, "No, man. Too much for me. Go ahead, Texas." Privileged to be chosen. Nona is the first one to meet Mr. Seymour. Pierce Kiereek Seymour. My firstborn grandson.

Amazing experience. Not like giving birth. It's different somehow. Unable to be defined. A precious and extraordinary event. Number one on my list of greats.

Less than a week later, Fletch gets kicked out of St. Matt's. Selling fraudulent bus passes he manufactured. He's a techie guy. Computer software's his expertise. The frantic fear of alone begins to congest my thoughts urging me to keep him close.

We move in with friends. A married couple who left the program a few months ago. She's a pill head. After breaking the well known and fundamental rule of associating with people who use, the typical consequence occurs.

Within the week I'm swallowing borrowed handfuls. "Give me a few more," I ask, "I'll take care of you when I get mine." I'm already on the prowl for my own generous scriptwriter.

Excited.

30

THE HOKEY-POKEY

You do the hokey pokey
And you turn yourself around
That's what it's all about.

My parents have lived in the big house for four years now. One brother is a customized painter, the other builds tailored kitchens, and the third does specialized landscape. These things in addition to my father's position and their inheritance money, enabled my folks to build this elaborate structure at a fraction of the cost. Their plan was to enjoy it a while, then sell it at a healthy profit. Not wanting to sacrifice the dream, a few poor business decisions, and the 2007 collapse of the housing market left them in a short sale. Thank goodness they have the house in Lake Placid.

The vacant mansion is in limbo. Azlynn's living in a two bedroom apartment but her roommate moved out. I can tell she's overwhelmed with the bills and the baby. Fletch and I, Azlynn and Pierce are more than excited to move in the house until the sale is finalized.

Strange here. Kinda puts me in mind of a haunted house. Empty and eerie. The whole deal is crushing. Doesn't seem possible.

Still waddling around like a famished duck in search of food—no doctor, no drugs—or should I say, "Quack." I'm without transportation and that makes it rough. Besides, my license is suspended. Thousands of dollars and many classes are my only hope for a rewarding trip to the DMV. The sum total of these circumstances leaves me no option but to resort to old faithful. Crack.

The baby's in daycare and my daughter's at work all day. It would be much better to smoke when I'm alone but that's not when the door to this business revolves. Most cocaine addicts don't even wake before 3 p.m.. The entire situation proves extremely uncomfortable. In all the years I've used, my children have never seen me high. I do my best to wait till Azlynn goes to sleep before I start smoking.

Tonight she's taking too long. These rocks feel like they're burning a hole through my pocket. No honorable crack-head would leave their product unattended for this long. Not on purpose. I strike the lighter. When she knocks on the bedroom door I'm paralyzed. "Mom. Mom, open the door for a second. Where are you?" I pull the door open but can't even make eye contact. She slams the door and storms away. She knows.

We only have a few months to stay here and so the entire time I'm in search of a rental that will take a disabled felon. Not many. Fletch is working and I still get a check. You'll never believe where we land. The same house that Bill and I lived in four years ago. It's over by St. Matt's and all kinds of druggies live in this area. In no time I find the perfect doctor and a ride to my monthly appointments. Convenient.

Eating pills is not enough and snorting them is out of the question. Cocaine is hard on the nose but at least it numbs. This stuff's way more hateful. My sinus cavity's torn up. Although there's a fortune to be made in the pill industry you never make a dollar when using. All you do is barter with people whose pickup date falls a few weeks after yours.

Come in contact with enough pill-heads and syringes show up. That's how it goes. The preparation becomes an all consuming fire. Extreme enjoyment. As if preparing an exquisite dinner for a loved one. Every touch is special. The shape of the spoon I use to cradle my baby. The size needle and how many units it holds. The color, consistency, and amount of product. The process provides an unusual flight of its own.

Roxicodone 30s—that's what I get. My favorite. The pill is a dreamy blue. On the streets they call them "Blues." I'm sure it's the same shade as a unicorn and every bit as impressive. Magical even.

I crush the pills in a dollar bill and scrape them into the spoon. Then I draw warm water into the empty rig. Slow and steady I spray it across the crumbled medication. Love to watch it dissolve and transform into a thick, smooth, liquid. Careful. Not too much water. Troubles melt away like the pill dust. I use a small tightly-balled piece of cotton to avoid waste. Don't want any left behind.

I'm shooting four pills at least three times a day. Finding the exact vein is complicated, especially when using regularly. The best ones are out of commission, bruised and swollen from previous stabs. Marks are everywhere. Hands, arms, legs. Ankles, wrists, between fingers or toes. Groin, chest, even neck. Wherever you can find a sturdy vein.

When the needle happens along a vein it shoots a red line of blood up into the sticky concoction. Like the ink from an octopus, the crimson stream fades the further it gets into the salty solution. This achievement sends bolts of glory from my heart straight to my brain. Invigorating.

Euphoria's just around the bend. The quicker I run the dope, the stronger the punch. If you're planning to get hit, why not make it an eighteen-wheeler and be completely smashed.

One slight movement can take you out of the vein and the whole shot will be lost, but anticipation makes steady hard to come by. Gotta stop halfway to be sure I'm still on target.

Tastes buds swell and flavor similar to aspirin fills my mouth. Then comes a dominating charge that removes reality from view. Faded blotches spot the walls, as if a faintly lit disco ball is turning overhead. I'm encouraged with enthusiasm. Stimulated, intoxicated.

Margins that were clear have lost their barriers. Soaring, sinking, flying, leaping. Above, throughout, within, about. The world swims. Deeper and deeper my soul dives. Like the jump from a bungee cord. Exhilarating.

Balance is a job my muscles seem to have forgotten. A disturbing mix of zest and fury. Just like I like it. An unparalleled energy. The intensity of the rush determines the distance between reloads. A factor that demands I push the limits. If some is good, more is better.

The savage hunger for high is equal to crack but the delirium of this enjoyment distracts from the feeling of immediate starvation. Wonder what the next rocket ride will cost me? Money, sex, my life? Doesn't even matter.

All words and an infinite timeframe could never make real the bliss found here. It's indescribable. Only an injection can tell that story. You'd think fear would steer you in the opposite direction. Instead it draws you in. A tricky evil that ignores logic.

What's meant to be a brilliant joyride can turn an unnoticed corner and drive you directly into a hollow pit of inescapable darkness.

Fletch hates the needle. He'd snort a pill or two—if I'd give him one—but I'm not the kind to go handing out samples. They're not Flintstone Vitamins. Last night we got in a huge argument about how I look. A mighty thin pincushion.

I promised him I'd stop. When my pal drops in with a box of new syringes, that ends that deal. Fletch is out back smoking, so he has no idea. I'm going to the bathroom to run these real quick before he comes in.

I decide to drop five pills. It may be my only shot.

I hurry through the process and hit a good vein—first poke. Nice. I run the whole amount. Before I'm able to remove the rig, my knees get weak. I cling to the sink's edge. Destruction pours over me. I'm stuck. No escape. What do I do? Make it stop.

Shock circles my skull till it transforms to terror. Howling moans, muffled shouts, all in a bizarre and rhythmic repetition. A volcano of nausea erupts filling my throat with stomach acid. I close my eyes but it doesn't help. Mud seems to be clogging my airway. Help!

Night creatures skip about with a tranquil, yet melodious cheer. Tiny trails of blood splatter, decorating the sink and mirror as I slide to the floor. Shooting up's a sloppy art. It leaves crimson evidence all over the walls of your soul, resisting every attempt at removal.

A loud knock comes. Too far away to unlock the door. Don't think I'd do it if I could. Fletch pounds and yells, "You better not be doing what I think you're doing. Open this door, Texas. Right now!"

A few more bangs and then comes the crash. He kicks the door off the hinges. Fright's transformed my expression, causing him to change his tone. He pulls me from the floor and sits me on the toilet. "It's okay, baby. I'm here. Right here."

Removing my clothes he places me in the tub and allows the shower to rain over me. He kneels beside me and holds my hand. Has to make sure I remain conscious. Once I'm coherent enough to respond, he lifts me from the tub, wraps me in his bathrobe, and takes me to the bed.

Twenty-five minutes pass before I'm able to stand and walk outside to smoke. Fletch is in the bathroom cleaning up the mess and breaking needles. We have our own bathroom but don't want the other roommates reporting to the landlord.

At the picnic table I light up. What have I turned into? Gross. No one I ever thought I'd be, that's for sure. My limbs resemble the pages of an atlas. I look old and hungry. Like I'm dying.

Through the dense humidity of the Southwest Florida summer night, I hear a voice. "I refuse to allow you to continue to spit in my face. Do you want to live, or do you want to die?" I recognize the sound. Louder than a whisper but definitely God.

If I were God this would be the end of the story. I mean patient hardly describes His behavior towards me. And then there's my poor parents. I'm an awful person.

I call my mother the next day and ask her to let me move to the lake. "I'm going to die, Mom. I know I am."

"I know this too, Texas." She says.

Throughout the next week Fletch watches me carefully. Still shooting. When the day comes he packs all my belongings in a U-Haul and drives me to the middle of the state. Lake Placid.

Letting me go is one of the hardest things he's ever done. Fletch is as dependent on me as I am the drugs. But he loves me. Loves me enough to let me go. To this day I know I'd be dead if he hadn't done this.

Chemical dependency is animalistic. It's been known to trample folks beyond recognition.

Mauled.

31

HERE I AM

Where is thumbkin?
Where is thumbkin?
Here I am!
Here I am!
How are you today sir?
Very well I thank you
Run and hide.
Run and hide

Cold turkey. Not a very nice way to go. Everything hurts. All day, every day. I wanna scream but my head may explode. I'd give anything for one pill. Just one. Detoxed many times but none of it compares to this. Opiate addiction is physical. My body feels like I've been mauled by a tiger. I've heard detailed stories of what others have gone through and this isn't close. Most have liquid running from both ends. I'm sick to my stomach but mainly I ache. All over. Even my eyeballs hurt.

It takes six days to get past my tortured state. Still not good, but better. Easier to do this in a strange area. I know no one here. Drugs are out of my system and out of my reach. The haze is lifting. My head's not throbbing with pain but unease jump-ropes through me without rest. I need to be doing something. Get busy.

The downstairs apartment is being remodeled. That means my parents and I share the upstairs. Difficult. A grown woman has no business living with her mother. Not like this. My parents are kind to me but they're tired. Underlying resentments. With good reason.

After a few months I decide to move downstairs. Here I'm enclosed by naked drywall and raw concrete. A dreary environment. I call it the "dungeon of despair."

Church is my only relief in this town. The praise and worship leader is fabulous. Power packed. Don't get how you can be so far removed from God and in one instant of honest worship, He shows up. As close to your heart as your rib cage.

There's a lady on Main Street who owns a bridal store. She just bought back the beauty shop next door. She was it's original owner. There's no real customer base but she needs someone to sit there. I take the job. Need out of this house. She's a wonderful Spirit-filled lady who knows my background and encourages me. I can tell she wants me to succeed. She teaches me many things I missed in school.

The more I know, the more comfortable she becomes leaving me here alone. There's a little Mexican store right across the street. After three weeks of twiddling my thumbs I decide to go get a Budweiser. Within a week I'm slamming four by 1 p.m. Don't like beer but I need the effect. I suck them through a straw as quick as possible. Get's you there faster. Learned that trick when there were no pills to shoot.

Lonesome and oppressed. I want to use. In the evenings I walk less than a mile to Publix. I spend my daily tip money on beer so I have to swipe the wine. Easy store to steal from. That's one of the benefits of small town life. With a big glass and a long straw I can finish a whole bottle in less than six minutes. Drinking is such a dismal existence. But better than sober.

When I'm unable to get more alcohol and I'm still awake, I steal my parent's stuff. I pour myself a big glass and add water to their bottle. You can convince yourself anything's okay when you're good and sauced-up. Deluded. I try to stay that way.

One day when they're having a glass of Pinot Grigio on the porch I come upstairs. I'm not drunk yet, so I go outside to say hello.

"Bob, doesn't this wine taste strange?" Mom asks.

My father looks right at me and says, "It's not full strength."

I remove myself from that scene as quickly as I can. I do my best to stay downstairs when I'm drunk but I know they know. They've been through this way too much. They are completely intoxicant-educated—thanks to me.

Eight seizures in the last two years. I'm on Medicaid so it won't cost me to see the doctor or get the medication. Still I won't go. As if not taking the pills means I don't have a seizure condition. Dumb. There's no rhyme or reason to when, where, or how I have them. The only consistency is that they happen when I'm asleep.

First seizure here and my mom insists I go to the doctor. "It's crazy how you'll take pills when you don't need them, but won't take them when you do. Why won't you take something that would help you, Texas?"

I find a local doctor and make an appointment. One visit and he suggests meds. I refuse.

A few days later my father calls the beauty shop. "Texas, I'm going to have to pick you up early today. Okay?"

"Sure, Dad."

One too many beers has me pretty tipsy. He'll know I'm drunk. Not wanting to face that turmoil I go through the drama of pretending I had another seizure. Don't do all the flopping just lay in the supply closet until the owner comes. Oh the mania.

She calls 911. At the hospital they prescribe Dilantin. I take the stuff to make my story believable.

Nothing brings pleasure anymore. The weight of past regrets and the dread of future results wait in ambush. Houdini himself couldn't outmaneuver these snares.

Tuesday morning a girl with bright red hair walks into the shop. She wants a color and cut. We have a great time laughing and talking trash. She loves her hair and before she leaves she tips me with a little blue pill. A Roxy. Like I always say, you can run but you can't hide. I take her phone number and by Friday I'm buying Blues. She's a junky so she throws in a few syringes—no cost. Right on time.

High keeps your mind active and your body brave. I start hitchhiking to the local bar every few nights. Don't know how my parents don't catch me. Luck, fate, denial. Whatever it is it's not a good thing. I'm trashed all the time. Even wet the bed a few times. Too drunk.

My parents are beaten down. Frantic for change but they can't make it for me. I can't stay here. Not like this. One day they call me upstairs and tell me I have to move. There's a psychologist at church who works at a sixty day, dual diagnosis program a few towns over. I met with him once so he knows who I am.

I hate programs but where else will I go? There's a long waiting list. Mom's going to ask if there's anyway he can bump me up. Maybe I have mental problems from the brain injury and this will help. It's only sixty days. Cakewalk. I could do that without shoes.

Detox is in Polk county, the Meth capital of the state. No matter where I end up, I have to get dried out first. Tried smoking Meth a few times but it proved to be a frustrating disappointment. No rush. What's the use of that? I took a big fat hit once and when I let it out I said, "You guys can keep this shit. Somebody call the dope man."

Been in Lake Placid less than a year. The distance between screw-ups gets shorter and shorter. Shocking. I use to make it a few years at least. Now I'm lucky to make it a few months.

Surprise, surprise, I got into the program. The van will be here to pick me up tomorrow. My three days in detox are quite interesting. I learn the effects of Methamphetamine. When you've been on it awhile, you do what they call the twist-a-flex. Strange body gyrations and jerks. Also, the substance will eat the teeth straight from your head. Glad it wasn't my thing.

Every time we have a smoke break, I notice this man. He stands away from the crowd. A gentle man who still has his wits about him. Never says much.

One afternoon when the two of us are the only ones outside I say, "Okay Dennis, so what's your deal? I haven't heard you talk in group and you hardly say a word out here either." I grab his cigarettes from the table. "You won't be getting these back until you tell me what's up with you," I say with a stern, yet compassionate, glow on my face.

He doesn't make eye contact and with a bashful grin he responds, "We have to get back in there for group, but I'll tell you about it the next time we come out."

He turns and heads for the door. Doesn't even ask for his Winstons. "Wait Dennis. Wait. Get these. I was kidding." I catch up to him in the hallway and push them into his shirt pocket. Our eyes meet and he smiles.

Group's over. Can't wait to get outside. Dying to know Dennis's story. When everyone leaves the area he walks over to where I am.

"So tell me, kind sir, how exactly did you end up in this joint?"

"Well Ms. Texas, I've only been home from prison four months."

"Why were you in prison?"

"Long story but I'll shave it down for you. When I was eighteen years old, some friends and I robbed a bank. Two people were shot in the mix of it all. No one died but I was sentenced to 60 years in prison. That was back when you only did 65% of your time. Thirty-eight years. Thirty of them in solitary."

"What?" I say. "Really? You've got to be kidding me. Why?"

"I hated being around the rest of the inmates. They're nasty, evil people. Always trying to hurt you or trip you up. I did things to ensure I stayed in the hole."

"Man, that's a long time to be alone." I shake my head.

"Now I'm a 56 year old man that's as scared as a little girl. The world has changed and I don't fit in. I can't even walk to the mailbox to get my mail without a drink."

My eyes fill with tears. "I'm sorry, Dennis. So, so, sorry. I don't know what else to say. Sure makes my problems seem simple." I drop my head in disgust. Then from the core of my being the same Spirit that keeps me trying for better, raises it's head and I say. "Well Dennis, ole' boy, that junk's over now. Time to get over it and get on with it. Can I pray with you."

"Sure can. Matter-of-fact, I'd like that." By the time he's released from detox he's smiling and talking. Not a social butterfly or anything, but one step at a time.

It's a gift. As long as I can remember I've had the ability to help people look on the bright side. Nothing I conjured up. Never wanted it. Used it, but mostly in the wrong way. Who wants influence? Then you're responsible for those who follow. Rather be an excellent sinner then a failed saint. Saints suck. Too judgmental.

This encounter brings new understanding to old beliefs. We're all held captive by personal deception. Other's blind spots are just as dark to them as my rotten chamber is to me. I'm beginning to wonder if I should stop fighting the bad and start celebrating the good. One day I'll find a way to just ignore the feelings until they pass. Before long, maybe I'll even be able to hug them. Appreciate they're importance.

Yeah right. Not today.

Stuck.

32

LITTLE CROOKED HOUSE

There was a crooked man, and he walked a crooked mile.
He found a crooked sixpence upon a crooked stile.
He bought a crooked cat, which caught a crooked mouse,
And they all lived together in a little crooked house.

Don't make it in the program. Get kicked out for kissing a 26-year-old boy. Don't ask. An entertaining and idiotic distraction. Once 40 passes, old begins to harass you. I was not the aggressor. Selfish none-the-less. For goodness sake, my children are close to that age. Foolishness. Anything to avoid my conscience. But none of that happened before three life-changing activities took place.

Each day we spend a few hours in a small group. No more than ten people. When new to the group, your first exercise is to write out a timeline and share it. All major events that affected your life. I'm older than most people here so it takes me a day and a half to present. As you tell your story, there's a person writing a tagline for each situation on a dry-erase board.

Revealing. Writing helps to determine the truth of what happened; sharing helps me own the facts and feelings. The last part is the best. When I'm done, I walk up to the board and erase all that's written on it. I like it.

The second function is this. "Write a letter to someone who you have unresolved issues with." Mom. In the letter I cuss and shout and call her all the names she deserves. She failed me and screwed up my whole life. I ask questions I want answered. I defend myself without concern for her heart. I shame her and blame her. It's her fault I'm stuck like this.

Don't mail the letter. Ends up writing it's enough. Gives me permission to make peace with unrealized pain. Fantastic experience.

Number three? One day as I listen to someone share in group I come to the unexpected realization that I deserted my children. For pride's sake I kept myself from seeing this realism. That night I call my children and ask them to forgive me for abandoning them.

"Wow, Mom. You've never said that," comes Azlynn's reply. Shows me the importance of this request. Glad to bring healing.

Shameful parting, but my time in this facility is productive. God uses everything. In spite of my stupidity. Dad's on his way to get me. Back to Naples. St. Matthew's House is home once more. Trying to make my own way, yet again.

Like every other time I'm here, I'm happy. Fletch is back on drugs. When he hears I'm at St. Matt's he comes too. He tries to rekindle the old fire but I keep pouring water on it. Nothing in it for me.

Never saw myself as someone who used people but it's true. It started in childhood. I cared deeply for other's thoughts and emotions. Till the day I accepted that no one cared about mine. Then I figured they owed me. All of them.

Most men are ruled by one head and it's not the one at the top of their body. I conclude I'm not being used if I'm getting something from the deal. And other people? I just lump them into the same category the moment I think they're taking advantage. Makes me better than them. Smarter anyway. Only it's inaccurate. I'm just as cold as they are. What Daddy says is true, "The truth is true, whether you believe it or not."

Can't work because I'm on disability so I'm assigned a volunteer position at the center. Separating and organizing cosmetic donations. Soaps and shampoos, razors and shaving cream. Deodorant, brushes, towels and toilet paper. You name it, we got it. I love organizing and am doing a fine job.

At any establishment, following the rules is not a problem for me. Don't ask why the rules of life give me so much trouble. During the dayshift, I'm allowed to get the key to the supply closet on my own. One night I notice I accidentally left a bag out of the closet. Not wanting the clients to stash the stuff as their own. I head to the front desk. Different shift but they won't mind if I get the key. I'm protecting their interests. When I come back the attendant's returned. He's angry. "You are never allowed to go behind this desk. Not ever. I'm writing you up. You're out of here." Try to explain, but he's deaf to me. The next morning I'm discharged.

Azlynn and her son Pierce have an apartment. My oldest boy Jordan, and his girlfriend Jazmin, live there too—such a cute couple—they've been together since eighth grade. My two kids are respectful, responsible people, for the most part. And Justice? He doesn't know enough to be nasty. I often wonder how Bubba and I gave birth to these babies. Undeserved treasures.

My daughter comes to pick me up. While here, I was approved by Section 8 to receive emergency housing. A miracle. The program pays 75% of my rent. Normally the wait list is three years. I fill out the application and am approved the exact same day. It's a new county program for disabled people. They pay for a one bedroom. I'm okay with that. Less space, less cleaning.

Finding a place seems impossible. Nothing's changed. No one in Naples wants to rent to a felon, even if it is guaranteed money. I won't quit looking, relentless at whatever I do. I'll just stay with my children until I find a rental.

A community that overlooks my past. Yay! Lakeview Condominiums. Originally built as an apartment complex, in 2000 someone bought them out. An upgrade. Lighted fountains in the lakes, a hot tub in the pool area, and the rare tropical landscape were added. Then they formed an association and sold them as low-end condos.

Since the market crash, it's an eyesore. Rundown. The front gates are propped open because they no longer work by code, the fountains shoot water in all the wrong directions, and a legion of Muscovy ducks traipse around like they own the place. None of this bothers me. My unit has beautiful ceiling fans and crown molding. Even granite countertops. If they approve of me, then I approve of them—ducks and all.

Whenever my name's been on the lease, the spot's been nice. Got to keep up appearances. But this is different. My very own place, with no one to answer to. Never had that. Unreal. Another shot. It's all up to me. Choice will dictate my outcome and I know I'll get it right this time.

It's all coming together. It always does. God's favor. It's not something I deserve. A gift He gives, jus' cuz. I've had charges with concrete evidence dropped for no known reason. You wouldn't believe the amount of furniture or cars I've been given over the years. That God dude's crazy about me. It's great.

But it nags at me. Why me? No matter how much I mess up, He's forever drowning me in perfect provision.

Fresh brewed coffee calls me from the bed. The pot has a timer. A splash of half-and-half, and a solid pour from the sugar server Mom bought me. She brought it and a dozen other ideal items when she came to check out my new pad. Don't get how she still cares. I suppose I hate me enough for both of us.

I read my morning devotion on the porch. This way I can smoke a 305 menthol at the same time. Nobody's perfect. Dressed and waiting on the curb by 6:30 a.m. My ride comes and we head to the homeless shelter for thirty minutes of group prayer. Helps me stay in the right lane.

Alone's odd. Not sure if I like it. I need to learn to be okay with me. Just me. Positive I don't like that part. Getting used to it though. Single for the first time in my life. Almost a year now. No matter who or how I've disappointed, no one's more tired of me than me. Without a decent distraction my flaws jump, whistle, and wave their arms, all in hopes of reminding me they live.

My apartment's on the backside of the building and all my neighbors use. Of course. Smoking on the porch keeps the air inside fresh, but outside stinks to high heaven. Not literally. I overhear conversations of products and pick ups, pipes and parties. That's what stinks. No matter how sure I am and how hard I fight—I lose. Every. Single. Time. Captivated, allured, and obsessed by the pungent odor of freewill.

Starts as an innocent drink and ends with a needle in my arm or a pipe between my lips. This is when alone becomes a huge perk. I say who comes, I say who goes. It's my house and in here the power belongs to me.

Thought for sure this was my ticket out. How could I mess this up? I was offered a stroll down easy street and couldn't even get that right. It takes action to create a new ending and my actions continue to leave me bound and beaten.

Shaken.

33

FRIDAY NIGHT'S DREAMS

Friday night's dream, on Saturday told,
Is sure to come true, be it ever so old.

Years back, on the final phase of my first rehabilitation center—before the mall job—I worked at a small clothing boutique on Third Street. Third Street and Fifth Avenue are the crème de la crème of shopping, dining, and art in Naples.

I become instant friends with Angelina Ricci, a 55 year old Italian woman who works here. I'm only nineteen, but the bond we have is remarkable. I gain so much from this practical, yet elaborate, well-polished and tasteful woman. A class act. I'm drawn in by her coarse humor and well-rehearsed social ethics.

I share my entire past dealings with Angelina. Hardheaded, shaken, used and abused. All is of great interest to her. She never seems disgusted by me. I'm not her child and am on "the other side" of these distasteful and unacceptable events. We laugh together and cry together. An extraordinary and meaningful time for both of us. She loves me and I'm sure of it.

Though never stated, she's convinced all this occurred due to poor upbringing. Being raised by simple church folk ruined me. Lack of social standing and education are what keep me lamed in this life I've been fated. She's certain she alone can, and will, save me from this misfortune. (Realizing now that much of her view was dysfunctional and not in alignment with my true beliefs, still I have tremendous appreciation for all the knowledge she shared.)

A quick study. I become light-headed with transformed possibility. I feel accepted by a group that has always kept me on the outside. I'm careful to find relevance in each lesson. She takes me to the finest restaurants, pricey shopping excursions, and trips to live theater performances. Things I've never experienced. On frequent occasion, I spend the night or weekend at her glamorous upscale condo. I love Angelina with everything in me.

One afternoon at the shop—while steaming the wrinkles out of an outfit for the window display—in he strolls. He pulls the curtain that separates the back from the shop and says. "Is my mom around?"

"I don't know, who's your mom?" I shoot back.

"Angelina Ricci."

His expression is filled with charm. Keen, with the appropriate amount of flirt blended in. I smile. Luciano Ricci. About five foot eight inches tall and balding at thirty. Overweight but nothing ridiculous, 25/30 pounds. Dressed in blue jeans, sockless loafers and an untucked, button-down Polo shirt. The color a cheerful shade of pinky peach. Typical Naples' attire.

The naughty twinkle in his eye, combined with a little boy smile of hopeful sincerity, tempts me to pay attention. Mysterious. He's much older than me but a good guy. This kind of thing shouldn't be overtaking my mind. I'm a long way from stable. Besides I'm prohibited from dating until I complete the program.

Rebellion's an unmistakable force of exhilaration. Absorbed by charisma I'm eager to know him. Outmaneuvered by infatuation I suppose.

Luke's the head bartender at the largest, most popular club in the area. Cliffhangers. We don't spend much time together. His hours and line of work don't jive with the new life I'm after. We enjoy a few dinners with his mother and her boyfriend, trips to the pool or beach. Even an unreported evening at his place.

We have sex but not until I graduate. Luke won't do it. No matter how I beg. Not until I'm done with the program. He hates what I've been through and is very protective of me. The entire experience is beneficial. It heals me to know he cares more for my freedom than my body.

Soon after, a business decision requires he move to Seattle. The furthest place from Florida in the entire United States. Destroyed. Most nights I fall asleep crying. Listening to Gloria Estefan sing, Anything For You.

Twenty-five years fly by and out of the blue my brother Curtis brings him up. "Hey, Tek, you'll never guess who I ran into at the sushi bar. Luciano Ricci. He was stoked to see me. He asked for you. Matter of fact he gave me his number and said, "Tell your sister to give an old friend a call.""

I don't get his number then, but I'm delighted to hear he asked for me.

Tonight, the guilt from my most recent relapse brings the warmth of Luke's smile to memory. I wonder how he is? Maybe it would help for me to go out with someone like him. May keep me from falling further, faster. It's worth a shot.

I call Curt to see if he kept the number. He did.

Time has passed but that doesn't stop the sound of his voice from melting me. Am I losing it? Unsure. At the end of the call, I remind him to save my number.

A few pleasant conversations of remember when come and go. I haven't been back in town that long and my sobriety's gone again. Although he owns an alcohol distribution business, he's not a drinker. A dreamy joy has overtaken me. Not what I'd call a common feeling. Stuck on emotional rewind.

"Of course," I respond when he asks me to dinner. Same bold assumption. Distraction will help.

His confident wit brings me great pleasure. Just like the 80s. The Heat Is On. But time and distance have created more solid barriers then those that already existed. Well hidden shame chews holes in every aspect of our vague potential. He'd never get over the life I've lived. No way.

Eating wonderful foods at beautiful places and learning things my walk of life have kept me from. I'm beneath him on one hand and way above him on the other. He has no tolerance for the things of God. Unacceptable. I don't practice or preach them, but they're true. I'm positive of that.

The time between visits is dark and dry. Left to myself too much. There's lonely, empty, hateful regret, and untamed, risky, childish ambition. Too much to overcome or understand. Why would returning to the former even be a thought? No sane soul ever promised addiction was rational. Not! Still, that's where I run.

When we're together I ask rifling questions that expose his pain. I'm an excellent reader of fragmented words. Eyes and body language tell a story of their own. My friend has deep wounds. Wolves of rejection and failure have ripped him to shreds. There can't be a God. Not in his mind.

Where do you find the comfort you need, if there's no God? I don't get it. God is real. The reason I know? Every time I turn to Him, He's there. Smiling and nodding His head in compassionate reassurance.

My messy state of repair can offer no relevance to the truth. Me and my self-motivated solutions are failing. Miserably. I don't want my behavior to add to the lies he already believes. I know in my heart that God is the answer but I'm in no position to prove it.

The next time he calls I answer and tell him I'm using. It's the truth. Never been much of a liar, unless jail's involved. I know he'll continue to call so I turn off my phone.

His messages the next day feel tragic. Tears of humiliation burst on the scene, providing yet another excuse for high.

Same cycle. I throw myself into the drug industry. Escape mode. The best way to stay high is to keep your own supply. I have excellent credit with every dealer I know. A lifetime ago, Jo-Jo taught me an invaluable concept. "All you have in life is your word, so do what you say." And when it comes to this life, it's automatic.

My customers are people who only smoke once every two or three weeks. Not the desperate type. When they spend, they spend big. There's usually someone in their life they don't want to know they're using. Keeps them locked here. Love that part.

Six years, no license. Doesn't matter though. When you sell drugs, people ache to be the one you call for a ride. There are two grocery stores and a liquor store right across the street. The assistance program also provided me with a brand-new bike. When drugs are skimp and people are scarce, I climb aboard and cruise across the street.

My appetite to beat the system sends my shoplifting into an uncontrolled landslide. Although I get a check and food stamps, I can't go to the store without stealing something. A sappy sense of invincibility always has me grabbing at a filler.

When I'm in bold effect I hit all three stores. The bike basket gets so lopsided I can hardly keep the wheel straight. I drink until my eyes won't open, not without a persistent banging on the window. They always come. Mostly the hustlers. They know I know people. My house is always in pristine order—no drama, no bullshit.

You sleep with one dealer and they all want a shot at it. No worries. I know how to say No. A No awards more dope than a Yes ever will. Proven fact. But no matter how tight your game is, eventually you gotta give it up. There's a few people I sleep with. In and out. A hit-it and quit-it deal.

No matter how you lay down, the after-effect is the same. Every time you give yourself away, a piece of your soul goes too. I've learned to deal with it. Forget. Pretend. But on unexpected occasion, remembered reality sneaks in and beats the hell out of me. Little left to value.

Tonight my hookup's out of product. Happens sometimes. I hop on my bike headed for a bottle. Something to get me through the dead time. I feel the eyes as I walk toward the door. No stopping now. The manager takes hold of my arm. "Just a minute, ma'am. Can you step this way." Held-up.

Four years since jail but I'm back. The bondsman comes to get me on my word. I'm trustworthy. Remember Fletch? The sweet guy who kept me from overdosing and helped me move to Lake Placid? He's still around. Good fallout plan. Pay's my bond the next day.

My mental transmission is slipping. Too far gone to attempt a different direction. All or nothing—still wired that way. Once I get to this point there's no way out. Not for me. Reminds me of Butch Cassidy and the Sundance Kid. Cornered on a cliff, the posse closing in. With one leap they pull their knees to their chests and towards the river they fall. "It's too late now."

Running out of ambition and sick-to-death of failure. Why continue to work for something you'll never achieve? However many shots you're given, I gotta be nearing the end of my overly healthy quota. There's no fixing me.

Broken.

34

THE CUPBOARD WAS BARE

Old Mother Hubbard
Went to the cupboard,
To give the poor dog a bone;
When she got there,
The cupboard was bare,
And so the poor dog had none.

Four days awake. High out of my skull on whatever comes parading past. Been in my own place for more than a year. Intoxication's not the same. These days the truth shows up no matter how dense my smokescreen. The thrill is gone. It's true—drugs of any style, shape or size are unable to provide the slightest space of contentment. Self-hatred and disgrace have gained unrelenting strength. Numb's not possible.

The hunt for drugs that once brought purpose, now leaves a void as deep as the Eiffel Tower is tall. Whichever feel-good solution I throw at my heart, there's a vacancy. Something's moved out. Don't think it's coming back either. This game has no finish line. Everyone who plays loses.

My head stays active. That's what it's used to—no brain-work, no body high. Most think of druggies as lazy. Get real. We plow through grotesque barriers to make things happen, most of the time without food or sleep. Talk about dedication.

Some people climb corporate ladders, organize school calendars, or direct the White House staff. Others put roofs on buildings, paint cars, or represent defendants. But nine-to-fiver's don't do near the work this job requires. Weaklings. Wouldn't last one day in this field. The bustle of this life makes a three story mall seem calm. Even in December. Addicts aren't dumb either—just captured—caught in sin that owns us body and soul.

Yet none of these rationalizations will fix my immediate problem. How do I get more money at 5:46 on a Monday morning? And where will I find good stuff if the money does come?

I have court tomorrow. The shoplifting charge. I won't wake up if I fall asleep at this hour. "More, more, more," the insistent voice repeats. I wish my brain had a force quit button and not just for tonight. Quitting is my only option if ever I expect to repair my broken state.

There's a tap on the door. One of my neighbors. A guy who lives a few buildings down. He walks in with an uptight smile and drops sixteen pieces of dope on the kitchen table. He's too freaked out to smoke alone. Can't relate to that problem but I'm more than happy to help. Gets me through till court.

I walk to the bus stop at 7:20. There's a PortaPotty at the final let-off. That's where I take my last hit. Go without sleep for two days or better, and the public becomes irrelevant.

Sitting in court always sucks. Before the ants in my pants start to bite, I'm called forward and sent home. Postponed.

A month passes and one unfortunate evening I find myself hemmed-up. No drugs, no money. What used to be rare occasion shows up a lot more often. The guy who runs the local food pantry smokes rocks. Good for me. Keeps my refrigerator and cabinets well-stocked. It's late Monday night and my new court date will be here come Wednesday. I'm sure they'll give me time. Don't need food stamps in jail and there's always a stamp buyer. They only give half value and I'm not usually a half-value kinda girl, but right about now nothing matters.

Court comes and they put me off for an additional six weeks. No disappointment found there. Don't eat a whole bunch but after three days I need food. Jacky, the guy from the food pantry, got fired. Smoking crack in the freezer. Government assistance doesn't come through till next week. I'm hungry. Can't believe my life has come to this.

I pick up the phone and call my son. "Jordan, I thought I was going to jail last week so I sold my food stamps. I'm hungry. Can you help me out?" How humiliating.

"I got you, Ma."

Within the hour a pizza man shows up with my favorite pizza and a two liter of Dr. Pepper. My Jordan's a sweet boy. Doesn't even question me. Wouldn't want me to be embarrassed.

At 6:30 that same afternoon he comes by. Plastic bags hanging from each finger. "Here, Mom. This should get you through."

Luckily there's no dealers around and I'm pretty sober.

Through a shameful mask my face shines with pride. Still, I'm demolished. How can he be here for me when I've not been there for him? Incomprehensible. I hug and kiss him. Out the door he strolls with a tender expression of relief.

I go to the kitchen and start unloading bags. My unsettled heart turns inside-out when I discover what's inside. Kraft Macaroni and Cheese. Kellogg's Pop Tarts. Merita white bread, butter, and sliced cheese. On and on. All the things I fed them growing up. What starts as a lump in my throat leaves me sobbing on the kitchen floor.

My babies, my babies, what happened to my babies? My little boy's all grown-up. I'm useless. I'll never be okay. I hate myself.

Cried like this countless times over the years. Pain that's too immense to ignore. Death would be far less dreadful, no matter how it came. Who wouldn't choose high? I cry till the salt burns my cheeks. My existence is disgraceful. Sleazy.

★ ★ ★

Harmon's what I call a pretty-boy. Sweet job, luxury car, and a beautiful home just down the street. Well kept. The latest and greatest of everything. A Dominican man. He wants me but that's beside the point. He's given me a few twenties—paid my electric bill once. An ace in the hole.

It's 3 a.m. on big money Friday. The pound on the door startles me. I stash my dope. Too sketched-out to move at full speed. Still I get there. Could be a spender. I look through the peephole. It's Harmon. After work he went to the bar with his friends. He's sloshed. I open the door and he falls through, barely able to stay on his feet.

He stumbles towards me with those touchy-feely hands. You know the kind. The weight of his body causes me to wobble and fall to the couch. He's all over me. I struggle to pull a leg free. When I do, with all my might, I slam my heel to his chest. Twice. That sobers him up.

"Get the blank, blank, blank out of my blankety, blank house. Now!" I roar with the outrage of a threatened seal. Louder and louder until he leaves.

A week later, after a party at some chick's place, I decide he owes me. I have her drop me at his house. My knock brings no response. This has happened before. Too much Bacardi. I proceed to the back door. I bang and bang, so hard the window in the door cracks. Although his car is here, he's not. It's November and the temperature's dropped so I have on a jacket. This gives me a wise idea.

Off comes the jacket and I carefully wipe whatever I've touched. Evidence. Removing my shoe I tap on the injured glass until it falls through. With the jacket around my hands, I unlock the door and walk in. I look around. No idea what will sell, where to take it, or how to get it. But I'm already in, so...

I call Franco. A customer who does this kinda thing. Masks and gloves in place, he and his partner are here in what seems like seconds.

"Go to the van, Texas. Open the back doors and wait there. Anything funny, ring my phone once. Got it?" Within ten minutes they've cleaned out the place and we're gone.

Three quick stops and we pull up to his house with a ton of quality powder. They got the cash. I got the coke. I'm a master chef. At the stovetop I transform the soft powder into hard rocks. For a day and a half we smoke like Navajos. I feel bad. Difficult to get my mind off what I've done.

The party ends and I go home. Never hiked this trail but I know where it leads. What's gotten into me? That was wrong. Trying to make sense of this nonsense I determine it's because I have no man. That's the problem. No one to guide and protect, to keep me levelheaded.

Distorted. Everything's gotten that way. What am I growing a conscience? Major conflict of interest. Being alone shoved me over a new edge. One I don't know how to fall from. Spent most of my life as a dangerous mountain climber but I always kept someone around as a safety precaution. Independence is a valley I've been careful to avoid.

Twelve hours later the vibration of the door wakes me. I see the badge when I look out. A detective. I give the house the once over to be sure there's nothing illegal in sight. I open the door. By the end of the conversation he knows I'm lying. I can tell. Lack of evidence forces him to get gone. Now I'm not only out on bond, the cops are nosing around. Thin ice.

Come Christmas my jewelry's absent. Desperation's a barbaric enemy. In all my years of drug abuse I held tight to my jewels. What good are a few $20 rocks that leave you with no bling. Definite crack-head move. I've lost it.

High and dry again, I walk outside to see if I can get into something. As much as I look out for the losers around here, I oughta be able to get a few free hits. Before I reach the bend in the sidewalk the police rush me. Slamming me to the ground they slap on the cuffs.

"What's going on? What did I do? You have to tell me what I'm charged with."

The detective who questioned me last month stands before me when they raise me to my feet. "Burglary of an unoccupied dwelling, Ms. Stready. How's that? Take her away, boys." Shoved in the crudely familiar back seat of a Collier County Sheriff's car and hauled off.

At the station I'm booked in record time. No money to count out, no jewelry to list, not even a purse or cell phone. Plain old despicable me. Frail and frightened.

Empty.

35

TRICK OR TREAT

Trick or treat,
smell my feet.
Give me something good to eat.
If you don't,
I won't be sad.
I'll just make you wish you had!

Twenty days and the charges are dropped. No evidence. Didn't ask for God's mercy but I know that's what did it. He's wasting His time. I've resigned myself to this life. No way out.

I come home to an almost empty apartment. My landlord thought sure the housing program was through with me. He got rid of my stuff. Since the charges were dropped, he must replace all the things he trashed. Refurnishing will be a nice change. Luckily I had Jordan come and get all my clothes.

I'm frugal and particular. The owner's a Jewish man and has no problem with that. We dig through many bargain bins and clearance stores—search every thrift shop in the area. In the end my place is fantastic once more.

I think he knows something's up. This bothers me. Not for the sake of my reputation but because he associates me with Christ. When I got this apartment I went on and on praising

God. I was in a much better place and that reaction came naturally.

I wonder—is the good stuff God's grace or a technique of the enemy? Maybe he keeps nice things available so I won't accomplish my purpose. Dangerous when I'm focused—everybody knows that. If I were him I wouldn't want me on the right side either. Doesn't really matter, I'm beat down. Can't change.

Besides who wants to be a representative for righteousness in a world that thrives on irreverence.

If I don't cut this out, I'm gonna end up one of those ragged old ladies on the bus. The kind who talks to herself through her two loose teeth. Shoe soles barely attached. Behind her ear she wears a fraying, hand-rolled cigarette that awaits the next stop. That'll be me. Don't want to go out like that.

Loved every guy I ever dated. As far as I can tell. Except maybe the Arab, but I was way too high to read between those lines. Then there's the others. I had to be attracted, even when drugs were involved. Seldom have I laid down with someone who had no appeal. Until lately. Life's chaotic. Things that have always been legible are now written in an indecipherable script.

The other day I was in my room, trying to flirt a drunk Mexican out of his pants and steal his extremely fat wallet. Lisa, the girl from upstairs, was on the phone. When she heard me say, "Shazam," she was to come to the door and bang in frantic hysteria.

My windows are tall but only twelve inches from the floor. Perfect escape route for an intimidated victim. Evil plan, but a guy who will do anything for sex, gets no sex and no respect. Not from me.

I hear a knock but I know it's not her. Moments later someone's at my room window. "Texas, you in there? It's me, Jonas." The guy who was outside the courthouse when I was released that night. The one who swears I'm flawless. Him.

I strike my lips with my pointer, eyes demanding the man's silence. The thought of Jonas knowing what I'm up to is crushing. Warped. Where does my head come up with this crap. A few more knocks and he leaves. As soon as he's gone I dismiss the Mexican—wallet intact. My heart aches. Facts are assaulting the lies I hold dear. I'm no different. Just like the rest of them. A crack-head. It's true.

Lisa comes down. "What happened?"

Lisa—a lesbian with a crush. She squats at the abandoned apartment above mine. I'm bent, but not in that direction and she knows this. Barely even associate with girls. We met in jail years back. She'll do whatever I hint at. Cook, clean, sleep with someone for drugs. Don't know how she found the place but having her around is sure convenient.

I start to explain how shame and pride erupted into battle when I heard Jonas' voice, but I can't get the words out. "It's okay, Texas. Don't cry. Please don't cry. Everything will be alright. What went wrong?"

"I ask myself that same question everyday, Lisa. What the hell went wrong? What have I turned into? I don't even know myself anymore." Agony floods me with a brutal vengeance.

If you add them all up, I've spent years of my life crying. Years and years. Disappointed by others, disgusted with self, discouraged, devastated, destroyed. Tears too many to number. Don't wallow for long. Futile activity. Just get back on the grind. That's what I do. Always on the hunt for the great escape. But no matter where I run, there I am. Me—can't get away from her. Used to be able to avoid it, but the screams become too loud to neglect.

"Is there anything I can do? You know I will," Lisa reminds.

"No," I shrug. "I'll be fine. Thanks for letting me suck my thumb. I'm over it. If I hadn't gone all soft I'da had homeboy's wallet."

I don't feel sorry for myself. Not my style. I'm the one who got me here. I dust the debris from my brain and pick up my phone.

"Time to *make* something happen. Carry-on!" I say with a wink.

★ ★ ★

Twenty minutes later a dealer shows up. One of those white boys who swears he's black.

"Here. Only got a few pieces of hard lef, gurl. You can get 'um. Not like I ain't made ple'ney money off you."

"Good lookin' out, man. Whatever money comes through tonight, I'll call you. Promise."

"You better," he says

"You got soft? I'd rather run powder then smoke crack." I say.

"Naw, not right now. You tried Molly, Tex? I got some. Check it out." He pulls out a bag of crystallized powder. Crunchier than cocaine or pills. Reminds me of Rock Candy. Remember that stuff?

"What do you do with this?" I ask.

"Snort it, shoot it," he says.

"How do you know? Ever seen somebody mainline it?"

"Ev'ryday. That oughta do it for ya, Tee. Shoot dat," he says nodding his head in the direction of a pile he left on the counter.

"Let me get my works." I skip to the bathroom to get my shootings supplies. I fix it up, draw it up, and run it up—as quick as a child's vaccination.

Blood races through my body at twice the speed of a normal shot. Back and forth vision skips like windshield wipers that lack water. Hawks scream as if offended by the screech of an unrehearsed violin. Stars fall from the sky that's engulfed my kitchen. Objects shiver inside their outlines. My breath's heavy, as if oxygen has lost it's life force.

My mind soars in search of undiscovered mysteries far beyond the universe. Puzzled. Do astronauts know when their rocket's about to explode? The pressure, the noise.

Bones throb. Ears screech. My eyes build pressure as if they will pop from their sockets. I don't like this. Not the usual kind of scary.

"Good, rite?" I can't respond. I grab the counter. "Call if an'body need som'. You look out for me, I look out for you. Holla at a nigga," he says on his way out.

He's gone and I'm gone too. Shot straight from the planet like a misguided satellite. The three minute rush finally passes but the high lasts for hours. Awful. Dying to come down. Hate it.

Reminds me of taking Black Beauties back in the day. Never was into speed. I'm hyper enough. Can't tell you what's different about cocaine but it's not the same. Man, I need a bottle, a Xanax or something.

Jerry's a spender who owns some bigwig car dealership. His wife left him so he's smoking an average of four grand a day. Most of my time for the last few weeks has been spent with him. Not real attractive but at least he's well manicured. Each hit he takes he gives me one so we get along well.

I know what kind of sex he's after. I've denied him for the eight months I've known him—but the pressure's on—don't want him to go elsewhere. Not spending like this.

I give in. Only happens once in a while and he's lucky if I go two minutes. A small price to pay. So why is it I'm the one who feels cheap?

Thank goodness Jerry's gone. Azlynn just called. She's coming by—never does that. A neighbor's son from across-the-way comes over when he sees her at my door. His Dad's her godfather and they grew up together. I open the door and they both walk in.

"Hey, Gurl, so ya liv' in Fort Myers now? What'cha doin' for work? He asks.

"I'm the night auditor at a big hotel."

"I thought we were close, Azlynn. I consider you family. Tell the truth. I know you workin' at the club."

I stand there dumbstruck by confusion. Bewildered. "The club? What club?" I know the girl she moved in with is a dancer but Azlynn won't even let me in the bathroom when she's taking a shower. My mind keeps adding but the total's in the negative. So I ask, expecting to hear how ridiculous my question is.

"What club? Azlynn, are you stripping?"

Silence speaks volumes. Grief fills my lungs and bleeds from my mouth. My chest heaves as I fight for air. I drop my head and tears splash to my eyeglasses. This is all my fault. I'm a depraved human. I wasn't there in her childhood and I'm not there now. Too busy doing drugs to know what's-up with my own daughter.

"Get out, Clarence. Why'd you say that in front of my mom? Now she's crying. Jus go." Azlynn yells.

"I jus' got too much respec' for you to hear people talkin' trash. You my god-sister. Knock that shit off, gurl," He says on his way out.

I feel like I accidentally escaped from Alcatraz. Fearful. No idea where to run or hide. Gotta get a hold of myself. I suck up the tears and take a deep breath. Who am I to judge? This is my opportunity to speak into her life. Tell her the truth, Texas. Say something.

"What are you doing, baby? And why?"

"It's not that big a deal, Mom. I only serve drinks. I can't make enough money to take care of me and Pierce. I have no choice," she says.

"Azlynn. Don't believe that lie. There's always a choice. Always."

"Don't worry, Mom. I gotta go. I'll see you later." She heads for the door.

I grab her and pull her close. "I love you, sweetheart. I'll always think you're incredible. No matter what. You know that, right?"

"I know it, Mom." She closes the door on her way out. I drop to the couch. Can't take care of myself, what advice can I possibly offer her? Worthless words. No weight to them. Can't imagine those nasty men pawing at my little girl. If any more liquid comes from my eyes this week, my face will slide off.

Before I'm able to get too upset the ring of my phone calls for my attention. It's Jerry. "I scored and I'm just around the corner. Get us set up, baby."

Terrific. Just what I need.

Deception's a wicked artist. It's tools distort any standard of beauty. The work it does is definitely abstract. Nothing factual or precise. Just a bunch of unrelated lines that lead nowhere. My life portrait's become muddy. A sore sight.

Frightful.

36

CIRCLE OF LOVE

The circle of love grows wider and wider,
The circle of love is you and me.
The circle of love is growing stronger,
The circle of love is free.

May 20th, 2013. This date's imprinted in my memory. Maybe because I clung to it for dear life. Sometime in the last part of March, I made a rigid promise to myself. One that no doubt saved my life. "I'm leaving here on May 20th. No matter what."

My groovy ringtone wakes me from two hours of semi-sleep. Drank so much I passed out. Again. No peace found here. It's as if I've been chased by a tribe of wild Injuns. No wonder John Wayne called it shut-eye. All I did was close my eyes.

"We'll be there in like 40 minutes, okay?"

"Okay," I reply to my mother's nervous tone.

I push the sleep from my eyes, grab my glasses from the nightstand, and take a deep breath. Then I light a smoke. Right in my bedroom. Never have smoked cigarettes in the house. Not till last week. I'm out of here and leaving everything behind. I'm smoking inside.

A glance over my right shoulder reveals a frightful site. A man I hardly know on the pillow next to mine. Another never. Did we?

Whatever. That was yesterday.

In the bathroom I wash my face, brush my teeth, then sort through the last of what's going. I force my electric toothbrush and face cleanser into my night case. An over-worn beauty bag I won selling Mary Kay 18 years ago. Man, was life great then. Now, like me, the old case has an ugly existence. Only used as a last resort.

This is no time for remember whens, Texas. Keep it moving. Keep it moving.

Mental chaos sends me to the porch to regroup. The rude orange sun glares across the pond making my small tile porch stuffy. Loved this porch when I moved in but now the atmosphere confines. Brings to mind a crowded pigpen. I scan the neighborhood for any last possibility. Hey, you never know?

I roll the lighter till fire shows up, then suck in hard filling my lungs to full capacity. It's a two hour trip to my parents' place and there'll be no smoking in that car. Nope.

Am I crazy? What am I thinking? Oughta call and save them the trip.

A strange sadness nudges me. One that forbids change. I turn to find my six foot cactus standing there all tall and proud. It's been with me since it was six inches. Won't be taking it. Or my 46 inch TV. No cool and comfy 600 count Ralph Lauren sheets, or brown and blue clay dishes I bought from a wealthy friend.

My Italian leather sofa set, and the beautiful pictures that once hung in my parents' gorgeous home, I lost in the last jail encounter. Today all that's going is me. Me and my clothes. That's it.

I crush out my half smoked cigarette, brush off my losses, and head back indoors. The pungent odor of independence fights for my attention. Don't listen to your mind, Texas. It's good at leaving out the misery. Gotta get out of this hellhole.

"Wake up Max. My parents are almost here." He stirs about in protest. I don't stop to bother with him. Too much to get done.

Max has been here for the last three days. He showed up with a friend of a friend. The palm full of crack granted his entrance, his pocket of cash afforded asylum. Released from jail only 22 hours prior. Don't know or care where his money came from. Some things are definitely better left unsaid.

I'm sure he plans on camping out here when I'm gone. Enjoying the A/C and selling my belongings. No problem. I used him like all the others. That's who I am anymore. Do their drugs, spend their money, then put 'em to work. He packed bags, shoplifted food, even rode the bike three miles to CVS for fresh syringes. Cooked and cleaned. Would have dug ditches if I'd asked. No place to go and no access to quality product. Ideal friend. In need and useful.

One drugless afternoon, three months back, I decide to answer Mom's call. Poor Ma. Wonder if she's lost hope yet? With a slight frown I push the green button on the phone. My body's sore. Been up an hour and only now am I able to move without groan. When you go long periods without sleep the crash is painful, not restful.

After we shuffle through the pretty talk, I detect her usual inquiring tone. The one that brings reality close enough to slap you. Before she speaks, I say, "Mom, you might as well not say it. This is the way I'm gonna live and this is how I'll die too. God has turned me over to my reprobate mind. Isn't that what scripture says? Well, it's happened."

"Texas, you get up this minute and make a circle. Then every time you pass it get inside and ask God for what you need. Do it until He answers. Got it?"

"Huh?" comes my reply. "What kind of circle? What are you talking about?" She explains and I repeat. "Just make any kind of circle? Then get in it when I pass and pray? Not because I want to? Not because I think it's going to work? Just out of sheer obedience?"

"Yes, Texas. The Bible says we have not because we ask not. So each time you pass that circle get in and ask. Ask! Ask! Ask!"

Mom remains on the line as I collect pinecones from the yard. Being a PK (preacher's kid) I remember that seven is the number of completion. It's also the day of my birth. I gather seven and place them in a circle beyond the sidewalk outside my front door.

When I'm finished I raise the phone to my ear, step inside, and carelessly say, "God, change my heart."

"That's what it would take, Mom. A change of heart."

"Great," she responds.

My phone beeps. Call waiting. "Gotta go. Important call. Talk to you later." Click. And I'm off. Running in the same exhausted direction.

April pressures March into the past. All the while I'm in and out of the prayer circle. Sometimes on my way to get a bottle or cigarettes. Sometimes headed back from the parking lot, crack rock carefully tucked in bra. Barely there long enough to inch out the words. On occasion I find myself there in the wee hours. Knees bent, hands raised. It's my last hope, so I just keep doing it.

Mid-April cyclones through and I agree to enter a long-term discipleship program. Victory Mansion. The yuck's gotten deep. Can't be ignored. I swore off treatment of any kind years ago. A waste. Something's changing.

I call the place and convince them I want help. I receive the application, fill it out, and send it in. No availability. Not till the end of June. Because of my effort, my father agrees to house me until there's an opening.

Looking like a junkie. Heels cracked. Toenail polish chipped. Unheard of. I have scrapes and marks from falling down drunk. Not to mention discolored welts from missed injection sites. Ugh. Been here before.

Every fall is further. My sole focus—avoiding bottom. Reality's formed by elaborate illusion. The longer I use, the deeper bottom becomes. Does this mean I've never hit it or maybe I've fallen through?

My parents have an appointment in Naples on the 20th of May. The date's set. Feels like a dream or some kind of joke. Am I really gonna try this? Rather than contemplate, I just keep getting in the circle. Everyday life's the same. Deranged. Getting as high as possible, as often as possible.

What's changing? My desire. Hope sees light and my prayers begin to grow. Instead of just asking for a change of heart, I ask God for a new view. I ask for purpose and contentment. I ask to be saved from myself. The more I get in the circle, the more I find myself encircled.

Dad's knock comes and I plow through the items stacked at the front door. I fling the door open with unshakable determination and begin instructing.

"Carry this suitcase to the car, will you, Dad? I don't need that big box."

I point toward a duffel bag with hanging clothes draped across it. "All this right here is going too, Max."

I grab my purse and my Mary Kay bag, then scramble towards the red Explorer. When the car is loaded my father climbs into the driver's seat. My insides shake. Doubt rummages through a million excuses.

"Wait, Dad. Let me check the house one last time." Before he responds, I leap from the backseat and rush towards my apartment. On my way in I notice the tattered prayer circle. Ambushed. Halted by a legion of emotions. I straighten the pine cones and step in one last time. My final prayer is the same as my first. "God, change my heart."

I venture from the circle—not towards the house—to the parking lot. Whatever I left, is left. I have enough.

With hardly a wave in Max's direction I hop in the vehicle. He stands on the curb with a dismal look of amazement. Lips parted in hopes of increasing air flow. No one thought I'd go through with this. Distributors laughed and shoppers pouted. All in disbelief. My brothers sighed, my children shrugged. And Daddy? He did everything not to get his hopes up. But Mom believed. She always believes.

A few blocks traveled I realize I left my Newports. They're on the porch. Too late to turn back. Although I'm sure they would, I won't ask my parents to buy a pack. Guess I quit smoking today too. You know me—all or nothing.

We hit I-75 and heavy, nagging tears gush from behind my glasses. As they stream, relief melts over me like butter on hot waffles, filling each square of life's abandoned purpose. Three months ago I'd resigned myself to a lifeless outcome. Mom's circle-making response came with such matter-of-fact urgency, it left me no choice but to comply.

Surrounded.

37

LICKED THE PLATTER CLEAN

Jack Sprat could eat no fat,
His wife could eat no lean.
And so betwixt the two,
They licked the platter clean

Misery rises like a rowdy child's temperature on a summer day. Just happens. My usual pool of refreshment has a crack in it. The sort that leaves me desolate. Dry as an abandoned piece of white bread that's been left on the dock after fishing for perch. A waste. My whole life's a waste.

I call and call. Leave general voicemails, personal messages, even emails. Nothing. No program. Who will fix me? What if my parents tell me I can't stay? Don't blame them if they do. Where will I go?

Surrounded by doubt, I wonder why. Why am I so weak? Why did I start this? Why can't I stop it? Why, why, why?

Thoughts are closing in. Repressed and repulsed. Not to mention the mental withdrawal deal. I feel less, more often than not—less rational, less capable, less motivated. All-around less human.

After two weeks, my parents and I agree—Victory Mansion must not be the place. Besides something seems different.

Maybe I'm over it. Don't miss that zone or the high. The life-long job of avoiding my feelings afforded no payoff. Cocaine's never-enough-campaign kills its pleasure principle. Every darn time.

My finger's callused from pushing rewind. All out of do-overs. Need a fresh strategy. A whole heap of well-formulated lies to dismantle. If that doesn't sound exhausting, one glance at the cost of reconstruction is sure to depress.

I pray. Ask God to help me ignore my theories and see the truth. If I stay in this trash can, garbage will be what I'm left with. Can't stand that outcome.

Seems far-fetched to expect people who've withstood years of letdown to place their battle in someone else's hands. News flash. We're all in the same conflict. Survival. Everyone steps on unexpected landmines that leave them wounded. Dismembered even. Mine are as gruesome to me as yours to you. Somebody's always got it better and somebody's always got it worse. On this, every honest soldier can agree.

Objective and optimistic one moment. Next, anguish has me in a chokehold.

I'm done with drugs. Awful option. What on earth justified my previous conduct? Determined to never go back. Grateful my family hasn't disowned me. I can do this.

Moments later, defeat's inevitable. The disgrace of not living up to or the weakness of just giving in to. Either's possible. Both entice cunning demons of remorse that must be avoided. Hate this insane intellectual riot.

There's no such thing as a guaranteed ending. You don't come into this world knowing how it works. The most practical of people long for the unrealistic image of perfection. Perfect mate, perfect career, perfect house. And then there's choices, churches, and children. We want them perfect too. Fact is, this faulty perspective leaves the most brave-hearted soul exposed and defensive—wondering what hit them.

The gentle and confident voice of the Holy Spirit speaks. I know it well. It's been there all the while. "Sweet Texas. I'm glad you're here. Although it feels like it, none of this caught Me off guard. Trust Me. I don't demand perfection. Just hang out in the lifeboat I've tossed you, and I will draw you to Me."

Then there's the other voice. The one that screams, "Impossible. This is reality, not some fairytale. Be serious. Don't be so simpleminded you fall into a ridiculous hole of hope. Not again. Whoever's selling that illusion wants to fool you."

Early on I decide I'm the only one I can count on. Whether that's true or not, I believe it. If I'm my best ally, I can't afford to go swimming in an ocean of pretty little lies, now can I?

At twelve years old I lived in Key West. Suzette was a lady who went to our church. She became close friends with my mother. A special lady. The type of care she gave was undeniable. Solid.

My self-proclaimed godmother, she named me Sparkle. Over the years, when I'm not swallowed in drug dependency, I remain in contact with her. Something about her ministers to me. Never judges or condemns. Doesn't lose heart or try to correct. Love. That's what she does. And she does it well. She loves grungy, jaded, dysfunctional me.

"My Sparkle, God made you to shine like a star and one day you'll do exactly that. Believe me. You'll see. You have no idea how much God loves you."

So many errors and so little space to tuck them from sight. Who's to blame? Why didn't my mom love me this way? Is her giver broken or my taker off track?

I've got no room to talk. Didn't do right by my own children. A constant disappointment. To family, church, and state. But more than any of those—to me.

Too weary to inhale. Justifications are soaked and anger's been wrung clean out. Simple. The person who's drowning is me.

Maybe addiction's a symptom. The problem? Powerful and aggravated emotions. Condemnation, sorrow, or lust. Arrogance, discouragement, shame. They're all about me. An egotistical echo whose pain requires deep distraction. An endurance mechanism. Corrupted. None of it makes sense anymore.

Everyone has issues they'd rather not own up to. This leaves us each in the doghouse. Mangy. Plagued by behaviors and mindsets that mangle our outer coat of protection. My head needs grooming. A bath, a brush, a blanket. Promised myself not to think too long or hard about any of this junk. My logic's like a puppy. Needs a short leash.

Been at the lake for two weeks now and already Azzie's planning to come. Unreal. I refuse to authorize the belief that this is my tired and useless 99th chance. That won't help. Azlynn's a mother now and Pierce is crazy about his Nona. Gotta get right. This is a chance. The chance.

Great having my girl here. She shares with me about the strip-club. Her views are tight and so are her legs. Met plenty of girls who've worked this circuit. Jailhouse stories have revealed how they operate. Relieved to know her head's on straight. Suppose I'm lucky. Still the imaginary sight of her in that place brings torture.

She's in love with the wrong guy. Everyone's convinced but her. On again off again. Two years now. She's pushing herself to break away. I know the feud between fact and fiction. This makes my opinion valid. I listen. Give her permission to come to her own conclusions. Glad to be present to the moment.

Today's the day that counts. The only one that's workable. So I'm working it.

Somewhere in the course of the weekend she says to me. "Mom, if I could give you one thing, it would be the ability to chill. Let go."

Busy in the kitchen, I burst into laughter. "You mean what I'm missing is the gift of chill? I'll attempt to locate that one."

Although not listed as a spiritual gift, it's a must. Gotta learn to say, "Who cares!" Cared way too much for way too long about things I had no control over. This balancing act kept me the clown in a two-bit circus for years.

Then there's the excuse juggling. Need to knock that off too.

Drugs have distorted my intelligence and clouded my horizon. The former cover's been lifted, but the comfort of that behavior is far from gone. In the weeks to come I train myself to still my mind. Quiet the storm. Find a sense of ease in the middle of emotional anarchy.

I determine that God can definitely be trusted and I absolutely cannot. This act of faith gives me enough visibility to recognize that these obsessions didn't appear overnight. I practiced the old habits for years. Implementing new ones will take time.

Uncharted territory is hard. A real nail-biter. The path to transformation is often slow and tedious, but the benefits are genuine. They don't fade away or explode in my face. Not like the frenzied clash of before. No fury, no insistency, no big deal.

Like the 1970s Beatles' classic Let It Be, this cry for help requires I take my hands off. So I do. I say Sayonara to my cocky mental psychologist. Time to fully turn to the infinite source within. The Power that is. It's easy to figure where true authority resides. Effective results—they're a dead giveaway.

★ ★ ★

Lack of absolutes, mingled with more than I can handle, take me straight to the gate of my most valued conviction: Why fight a war I'll never win? Then comes the response my journey's been charted from: Find a way to enjoy your losses.

Years of foolish calculations make it tough to draw proper conclusions. If I don't have problems, I don't need help. If I don't need help, I'm independent. Independence is lonely and problems suck. How's that fair? Everyone longs to be self-reliant and stress free.

The key to an accurate view begins with the entire truth. Each of us is at an equal distance from perfection. Can't be concerned with anyone else's free-for-all. I must come to the complete realization of how far gone I am. It's the only thing I'm responsible for.

Appropriate fear is a critical factor. It's absence disables respect. Makes me bossy and careless. Removes appreciation for life. Death was my hope a few months back. Grace. The only

Step 1

explanation. Don't want to die. Not really. Another lie I bought into.

My only shot at freedom is established in the struggle to make peace with reliance. I'm meant to be dependent on an unseen force. Not what I'd call comfortable.

As I review my history, unquestionable evidence is there. It creates a distinct and recognizable picture. One I've not been able to see till now. I left home at the age of 17 on a trip to discover authenticity. To find the whole truth and nothing but the truth. A prideful and selfish venture I do not recommend. But the truth always radiates. Especially in darkness.

God is reliable, faithfully giving in a world of misgivings.

Evil brings death to everything that's substantial and pure. Even when it's not purposed to be wicked. But God gives a trade-off that's out of this world—His perfection for my sin. Understood and believed this at the age of five. So why did my life take this course? Never found rescue. I thought understanding why I did what I did would give me the power to be different.

Guess what I'm learning? "Why?" is irrelevant. That question may never be answered. I'm the one who beat myself for every flaw. No wonder I search for escape. Restrained and ridiculed by a harsh and troubled psyche. What I need saving from is me. My way. I'm over it already.

Finished.

38

IN THE OVEN

Pat a cake, Pat a cake, baker's man,
Bake me a cake as fast as you can.
Pat it and prick it and mark it with 'B'.
And put it in the oven for baby and me.

Headed back to Naples. Dad's driving. Court. Same old shop-lifting charge still pending. After ten minutes of contemplating my best bet, I ask. "What should I say to these people, Daddy? Judge Harold knows me. Well."

I begin to rehearse my thoughts aloud. Hoping for insightful input.

"I think you should throw yourself on the mercy of the court. Let God do what He sees fit," Dad instructs.

I stare out the window. Sorting through words. Don't believe in schmoozing. Just careful to say what is factual and beneficial in the same sentence. If there's proof enough to get me before the judge, silence may be my most practical defense. No calculated fallout. Don't even know what I'd like to happen. Winging it.

I ask the Lord for a clue.

"Tell the truth, Texas." That's what He says. "It will set you free."

"Free? No jail?" My heart flutters.

"My intent isn't to keep you from jail. It's to help you be finished with this lifestyle. The truth is where the race begins. Sit honestly in the darkness you've created until you see light. Don't avoid any of it. Be real about who you are and where you are."

The rest of the trip Dad and I discuss various topics. Things to amuse or divert. When we arrive at the courthouse tension and doubt fight for my acceptance. I dismiss both and continue to ask for the ability to chill.

When my name's called I approach the bench. Judge Harold says, "Ms. Stready. How are you today?"

"Different," I respond. "No justifications or plans. I'm done. Been on and off drugs for 27 years. I'm tired of this reputation and this town. Cut the place lose. Left empty-handed and moved to my parents in Lake Placid. Please give me the opportunity to pursue different."

"Ms. Stready, you've been around enough to know, I've heard every story that can be told. I hope you stick to your word for the sake of your life as well as the law. But I must sentence you within the guidelines. You will be remanded to custody for 60 days, all credit-time-served. To be followed by one year of county probation. Good luck to you, Ms. Stready." The gavel strikes.

"Can I hug my dad, Your Honor?"

"Go right ahead." The bailiff walks me to my father.

I throw my arms around him. "I love you."

"I'll be here when you get out, baby." He kisses my forehead.

Escorted to the back and taken into custody. Incarcerated.

Sure seems the same. Except I'm happy. The sentence is more than fair. Fifth misdemeanor petty theft. Should have been converted to a felony after three. That would mean prison. Grateful. I want liberation and this stay will reinforce my commitment.

★ ★ ★

The church ladies still come. All these years. This time I'm excited to see them. "Left it all, Ms. Sherry. Gone from here. I'm living with my parents. Had to come do this time, then I'm finished."

She's heard the promise before. What's changed? This is my first week in. Operating out of desire for, not in result of. I arrived at this new perspective by remaining in the lifeboat. So much easier than trying to save myself.

I've determined to begin my memoir. Joked about it many times throughout the years but lack of positive conclusions kept me laughing. Besides, what do I know about book writing? Can't spell, don't know diddly about the computer—heck I'm not even a reader. Still, something inside tells me it's relevant. Part of a higher purpose.

I've made up my mind. Gonna use one of Jo-Jo's rules. "If you don't know, just act like it." I'm going to act like a different person until I become one. A writer.

Mom sends me The Circle Maker by Mark Batterson. That's where she learned about praying circles. To make a personal prayer circle, I rip seven pages from the jailhouse rule book. Don't have any paper yet. I draw a star on each one—for Texas, the Lone Star State.

Every morning and every night I place them in a circle and step in and ask for fresh desire. No magic's found in this process. Just reminds me to stay dedicated. Keep asking.

Praise is at a max. My outlook's becoming crisp and clear. I talk to and pray with many people—as usual. But it's not the usual. I've taken an about-face. God's honoring my insistent prayers. The emotional evidence is proof. I'm operating from my heart instead of my head. Effective.

I want to be solely reliant. Time to latch onto an active solution. My pattern's ineffective. Rusted and decayed. Loaded with filthy lies. Finding Divine insight requires total abandon. My former habit of self-cleanup makes it hard to sit with the stains. But I don't have a choice. Wiped out my right to listen to me.

Heaviness tugs at my soul on occasion. Suppose that's okay. The old, what-will-this-require question, floats to my mind's surface. My entire life's been spent holding on by the skin of my teeth. Without success, I might add. Now I'm fastened to a secure anchor. Don't have to worry with my grasp. The effects aren't dependent on me. A courageous and convinced kinda cozy.

God isn't out to punish; He wants to protect. He doesn't want to fix what's broken; He wants to replace it. What matters to me does matter to Him. Can't understand His methods because He isn't human. They're beyond me. If I can figure it out, it's not faith. All new concepts.

Beliefs are blended. Deciding what's accurate feels hazardous. My head spins around true and false. Comfort and confrontation. Can't tame my wild reasons. Instead I boogie to the beat of whatever stampede they start, content with the notion that, in the end, I'll be the star of this rodeo.

The course sound of the robotic door alerts the dormitory each time it opens. Customary response? Poke your head out and see who's there. Boredom brings out the nosy in you.

It's Bayshore Betty. Bayshore Drive is the place to pick up prostitutes in Naples. They call them "Bayshore Whores" And Betty's the queen. Been here on countless occasions. Fragile, shabby, and drained. That's how she looks. Don't think I'm superior, but not one of them either.

Not until today. Make-believe's dead. Fact's are apparent. Truth glares straight through the curtain and reveals my deceptive stage props. That is me. Different character, same performance.

She drags her green plastic mat along the floor. The walk of shame. Not dumb enough to think everybody loves me, but they do respect me. I do my best to avoid people who require assault. Verbal or physical. Not my thing. I'd much rather outsmart you. I stay out of the hubbub, say it like I see it, and I care. Always my same self.

I walk over and wrap my arms around Betty. No one's shocked. What can I say—I'm a hugger.

She's too coarse to drop a tear. I draw back and look at her face. "Aren't you sick of this? I sure am." I pull her close once more. Longer than is comfortable.

As she makes her bed she begins to cuss about why she shouldn't be here and how her sugar-daddy should have posted bond by now. Same stuff all newcomers rant about.

"You good?" I ask, amazed as I watch the theatrical mask cover her indented face.

"Yeah, I'm straight, girl. Great actually. I ran across a good sucker. And you?" Before I can respond her doorway's piled high with curious criminals.

"I'll let you get set up. Talk to you later." I leave.

Doesn't matter how many times I come here, it's never okay. Can't fake it like that. Instead of wrestling with denial, I chose to cradle my flaws. Although that strategy didn't work well either. Left me every bit as tapped out as the next loser.

An hour later Betty peeks into my room looking depressed. "I'm freezing. You got an extra t-shirt or some socks?"

Arms filled with shower supplies, I shrug. Excuses are high-stepping it in the Me Parade that marches through my mind. Self-preservation mode.

"I'll check it out when I get back." Never been a hoarder or a fool. I know the scuffle. These chicks'll stomp on your neck if you let them. Always trying to get over on someone.

She turns to leave and His whisper comes. "You have three shirts that were given to you. She needs one. Are you doing things your way or Mine?" Without hesitation I put down my things and dig around till I find a shirt.

"Betty! Betty! Come back. Here. Be warm, chick." I smile, collect my belongings, and move toward the showering trough. That's what the lesbians call it. Nasty. These people act like animals, because that's how they're treated. By themselves and others. The place is a barnyard.

After dinner we have two hours of lock down. Shift change. I spend all night reading. A common routine. It's quiet then. Makes the night fly by and sleep erases the day. Didn't read three books before jail. But in here it separates me from this hamster wheel existence.

The night crew announces the evening roster. "Supplies! If you need toilet paper, pads, or tampons—line up. No congregating around cell doors. If it's not your room, don't go there.

Showers close at 10:30, girls. TV's are on now. Don't come to the speaker asking dumb questions. Let's have a good night. No drama. You're off lock."

The offensive sound of forty steel doors popping at once rings through the empty dayroom. A hunting echo that's unmatched. The sound vibrates your bones. I reach for my two stashed oranges. Each morning I trade my valuable breakfast items for five oranges. I consume three at 4 a.m. and save the last two for now. This morning one had a rotten spot. Chucked it. At least I have one left.

Avoiding shakedown's the trick. When a new shift comes on there's always the chance for search. I eat mine as soon as they get here. If you're caught with contraband you're locked down for the evening. Seven o'clock on. The best time here. Everyone's awake and cheerful. We're children of the night. Our clocks are behind.

I sit on my bed to enjoy my valued evening treat. Milky Ways and Honey Buns make Tex-Ass too much. Only 47 days to go and no drugs to drop the weight. Better stick to my oranges.

Betty's loud voice rings through the dayroom. I think of how hungry I was my first night. The Holy Spirit says, "Give her that orange."

I argue, "Really? Really, God? Damn, man, I'm doing it all. Staying upbeat. Keeping my mind focused. Praying circles. Is it ever enough? Now you want my orange? Really?" I call her to me and grudgingly extend the orange her way. She grins and grabs it.

"This is too much, Lord. Way too much. I'd like to promise that selfless giving will one day be easy. But not today. I only did that because I had to. Don't want to screw up what I've got going."

"You had to?" He says. "You never have to. And you're not the one who has this going. I am. Poverty mentality. That's what makes it hard for you. Here's the truth: You're a citizen of My kingdom. Here to accomplish My will. This affords you access to all the riches of Heaven. You may not have everything you want but you won't be without. How 'bout you smoke on that awhile."

I laugh out loud. The King and I are becoming close friends. He speaks to me in the same way I communicate. Nice. That's what relationship's about. A bond. Knowing and engaging one another. A developed honor and discernment.

Ease overtakes me. You lead. I follow. I'm Your representative so You supply my needs. Think I'm getting it. Sweet deal. Even if it does leave me orange-less.

Where's my book? I reach my arm beneath my bed and shuffle through my plastic bin. My hand runs into something cold and round. I know what's where, at all times. Keeps me out of trouble.

Is this an orange? I glance over the edge of my bed. It is! Unbelievable. *Nice navigating, Dude.*

My new Captain's mad about me, and He knows the shortest way to get where I need to go. In addition to that, He has all the necessary power to keep things working in my favor.

You got it goin' on, God.

Hot.

39

It's a Shame

Take me out to the ballpark, take me out to the game.
Buy me some peanuts and cracker jacks,
I don't care if we ever get back.
For it's root, root, root for the home team,
If they don't win it's a shame.
And it's one two three strikes you're out,
at the old ball game.

My return to Lake Placid is a festive event. Gratitude dances in my heart. Such optimism. The responsibility of adjustment brings pressure but it's unsafe to look too far ahead. Gotta relax into the now. Enjoy today. An absolute essential.

Write, write, write. It's all I do anymore. Not so much for the reason of helping others. Do it more to document my brain activity. When I talk to people who have their lives together I realize I don't hear thoughts properly. Too self-absorbed.

Taking note of this demands evaluation. The process brings enormous satisfaction. Shows me how detrimental my behaviors have become. Keeps me active, accomplished, and amazed. Rewarding. Just what I need.

What I once considered normal, now appears ludicrous. We're all motivated by defective perceptions that influence our belief system. Stuff we refused to give up. Destructive conclusions we accept as truth. Wonder if this book will help the obviously blind or maybe those who swear they can see. Never been prejudiced. It's for any cornered soul that wants movement. Mainly me.

I was a difficult child. Still hard to figure. Don't get why God made me who I am and drugs have worked hard to exaggerate my hostility on the matter. I've spent far too many years coming up with scandalous verdicts that always end in self-betrayal. I want to learn to be faithful to me. A custom that requires repetition.

My personal mix of mind hurts most when it comes to approval. It leaves me with nothing but a smoldering pile of angry assumptions. A hot mess. Self-acceptance is all that will quench this fire. Something within provokes me to establish peace with who I'm designed to be. Find my own security. Don't need outside okays.

I want people to respect my identity. Appreciate who I am. But somehow I don't consider theirs. Double standard. Everyone isn't like me, and they're not meant to be. I must learn to welcome individuality.

Can someone else affect my choice? Not if I don't let them. I used my mama's flaws as an excuse for years. The blame game. A system I thought was foolproof. Didn't work so well—in the end, I became the fool.

My fault-finder's out of gas. Can't stand people that won't own their share of the problem, yet that's who I've become. Too much psychological wreckage. The best way to start again is to juice up with humility and steer my wheel in the opposite direction. Become the best me I can be. Not responsible to repair or refuel anyone else's get-up-and-go. Just mine.

With a clear head I review my history. Elementary insights resurface. Bad consequences accompany bad choices. Hurt feelings need healing. People who need forgiveness should be quick to give it. Important fundamentals to redevelop.

Drug addiction forced me to plow through a barren wasteland in search of counterfeit treasure I thought would bring profit. Deceived. No telling what I'll achieve in this new way of life. Won't take much to outdo the former. Definitely no success found there. Discovering why I chose these things won't fix them. What and how, are better questions.

What do I do next? How do I become whole? That's where my consideration should be. I'll use my old skill of focus to hit my new target of freedom.

What? Anything it takes. How? Without reservation.

Even if the entire world remains the same I'm going to unearth my true potential. I'll sharpen my aim by changing why, to why not. Bull's-eye.

Been here five months. Still writing well and feeling fine. Both Azlynn and Jordan have been over to see me. Even saw Justice last weekend. Can you believe I'm actually out of that life? I can't.

We live on a dead-end street. Houses line only one side of the road. Pretty rural. The downstairs is finished now. The Dungeon of Despair's been replaced by the Haven of Happiness. My cellphone rings. I pause from my work to answer. It's Azlynn. We talk every day. Love it.

I stand to stretch my legs. Been crunched in front of this computer since 5 a.m. I stare from the window at the easy flow of the lake. My apartment's on the backside so the water's just beyond the walkway. Tranquil. Like restful sleep.

The corner of my eye detects movement. Shocked by the sight, I say, "Azlynn, there's a cop coming to my door." Before I can swallow hard I see another uniform. "There's two of them. What on earth? I better go."

"Okay, Mom. I'll call Gram and tell her what's up."

The knock comes. My pulse throbs in my eyes and sweat beads on my scalp. I open the door.

"Good morning, ma'am. We're looking for Texas Stready."

"I'm Texas. How can I help you?" I say as I straighten my nightshirt.

"We have a warrant for your arrest."

"What? There must be a mistake. I've been here for five months and haven't broken any laws."

Just then, Mom turns the corner, fear alive in her eyes.

"What's the warrant for, officer?" I ask.

"I'm sorry, ma'am, it doesn't say. Let me see if I can call and find out."

He turns to activate his radio. I can hear the sound of Mother's voice. She's close but the noise of her speech is muffled. A distant quiver. She asks the other policeman questions and maintains that their information is inaccurate.

Even if it's a mistake, I've already accepted the fact that I'm going to the station. I know how it works. No matter who's at fault, a warrant means jail. Eyes glued to the officer, dread saturates my skull. This is worse than a bad dream. More like a stab to the chest.

"Something to do with cocaine sales over in Collier county. That's all the info I have. Can you come with us?"

I want to say, "Hell no, I can't come with you," but I know it's not a real question.

Mom complains, "Can she at least put on some clothes."

"Yes, ma'am. She can step into the closet but don't close the front door."

I walk from the closet too spooked to cry. Outside the door I cross my wrists behind me. Bound and led to the patrol car.

Never gone down like this. Always caught in the act or turned myself in. Not much of a runner. Just face it as it comes. That's me. But today, everything inside promises I'd run like the devil if I could get free.

It's like I just gained consciousness after a seizure. Weak and confused. Floored. No idea what's happened or how to make my way back into the now.

Highlands County is an old-timey jail. After two days in this decrepit torture chamber, I'm transported to the Naples Jail Center. My charges are: two counts of sales or delivery of cocaine, and one count of possession with intent to sell. Each charge carries a maximum sentence of fifteen years in prison. Worst case scenario.

Won't happen. Although five years prison per charge, run concurrent, is a likely possibility.

Nothing's different here. Except me. I'm disappointed but stable and courageous. God will deliver me. He's done it on plenty of unmerited occasions. Been almost perfect since I dipped from this scene. I deserve rescue. Wouldn't you say?

Within weeks, my bunk becomes a prayer palace with a revolving door. An effective one, I might add. The army's in place and I have the advantage that comes from close contact with the Head Honcho. Most requests involve major life crisis. A heavy sword to swing but these battles are critical.

The real responsibility's on the Commander-in-Chief, and He can handle it. God's plan provides a wonderful remedy for each and every life of missed opportunity.

In the afternoon I speed-walk around the open dorm singing, No Place I'd Rather Be. It's a worship song I learned at First Baptist Church Lake Placid. It's no performance, I truly mean it. Astounded by this swap. Alarm for acceptance. I'm over being scared about what will happen. I'd rather have close connection with the one true Source and in jail, than to be anywhere else on earth. Any good thief can tell you that's a steal.

After three prolonged months and numerous discussions with my public defender, I learn the details. This is the result of an open investigation from a year back. There are video and audio recordings of each transaction. Pegged. Absolute evidence.

It's miracle time. Or could it be that this is where I'm most effective? Hope not.

Two months before I'm in front of the judge. He sentences me to a year in the county. Can't believe it. What about the miraculous? Deliverance? Complete forgiveness? Disaster triumphs again. The judicial system's warped, and the God program appears the same at times.

Then I hear the Holy Spirit say, "What happened to our exchange? Alarm for acceptance, your will for Mine? Don't speak about it, be about it. Isn't that what the brothers say? Haven't you learned anything? I *did* rescue you. So act like it. Buck up. Think of how this could have gone."

"It's true. It's true," I burst into praise. "Thank You, Jesus. Thank You." I'm sure folks think I'm a lunatic but I could care less. God has been relentlessly kind to me.

Human intelligence doesn't give me the understanding to make sense of it all. It's important I understand my rightful position. No need for me to be the boss, instead I'm learning to focus on the One who is in control.

My sister's dying. No one wants to say it, but it's true. A herd of wild apologies trample me. Death seems more suitable to me than her. My insolence has kept our relationship from proper advancement. Painful. I'd switch places with her if I could.

Dori and I have only been together on a handful of occasions. Not anywhere near as much as she's been with the rest of my family. Still, an undeniable love for her lives in me. Last year's terminal cancer diagnosis conquered me with grief and regret.

The family's going to California this week to be with her, just in case. I'll call Mom's phone and talk to Dori on Tuesday. How pathetic. Not enough. Tragic. But better than nothing.

Yesterday's gone. Stay in today. I keep repeating it, but some losses require more to get past than others.

Life and death. May miss both. My daughter's pregnant with her second child and her due date is two weeks before my release date. Although my life has pivoted atop some sordid sense of entitlement, I seldom feel justified or worthy. Far too aware of my wrongs to be angered by injustice.

I've been given so many opportunities. Justice would mean getting what is due me. Can't say that deal's crawling with positive possibilities.

I'm on the down slope. Anticipation. That's what's getting me through. Eager to get back to living. My whole life awaits me. This time has been hard. The longest stretch I've ever done. I'm tired. Ready for this to be in the past.

Impatient.

40

ALL THE WAY HOME

This little piggy went to market,
This little piggy stayed home,
This little piggy had roast beef,
This little piggy had none.
And this little piggy went wee, wee, wee,
All the way home.

Ten months of stuffy accommodations and sucky attitudes. Time's up. I'm outta here. I sit on the bench by the flagpoles anxious to see the Explorer round the corner. When the custom red catches my eye, time halts.

A much taller five-year-old comes flying down the sidewalk, beautiful bronze dreadlocks bounce around his head. Arms stretched fully my way he screams, "Nona, Nona. My Nona." He's my biggest fan. Unconditional, undeserved, unrestrained love. Pierce is guilty as charged.

Next I walk to my teary daughter who extends to me her bundle of new life. Baby Solace. Holding him feels burdened. Stiff. Almost uncomfortable. Can't believe he's real.

I feel like Dorothy in The Wizard of Oz. After a long journey through a mysterious and life-changing landscape, I'm impatient for home. I breathe in the scent of my new grandson and pull my Azlynn close.

Then it's Mommy. I squeeze her as tight as I can and kiss her whole face. Whenever I'm in trouble, no one cares for my needs and feelings as good as Mom. From now on, I will use the time spent here as a constant reminder of this.

My brother Curtis and his girlfriend, Wendy, meet me at the store for coffee and congratulations. Then it's off to Buddy and Dorothy's where the rest of my family and a delicious breakfast await me. Azlynn, the children and I, will be staying here until we can find her an affordable apartment to rent. In Naples, most places in her price range are pitiful.

Pregnancy closed the door to her club career. The poisonous relationship she was in brought Solace to life, in more ways than one. That's over too. She's single. God is faithful to bring His best from our worst.

I'm on drug-offender probation for six months, so I decide to stay with her and care for the baby during this time.

Excitement settles, but only for a moment. Jordan and Jazmin are engaged. Happened while I was incarcerated. Thank goodness they were adamant about waiting until my return for the ceremony. The wedding will be held on the wooden deck, beneath the flawless and exotic landscape around my brother's pool. This means my curfew can't keep me from enjoying any of this marvelous event. Spectacular. I'm loaded with joy and admiration for the two of them.

I sip on a few drinks at the wedding but nothing out of hand. It's a celebration and there's so much to be celebrated. Besides, alcohol's never been a persistent problem. My brain and body are in a whole new place. Exactly where they belong.

This town has a way of keeping the former, front and center. For me, anyway. Old injuries ache from time to time and lifelong deductions are demanding and over-talkative. Will I ever find a steadfast sense of contentment? I sure hope so.

The need to correct is a prominent branch in my family tree, bringing yesterday's harsh requirements into today. Hesitation and frustration are expected. Let's face it, my reality's been a continual letdown. To all of us.

Doubt's agitated poke was dormant for ten long months. It's re-entry into what I thought would be a gentle transition of restoration, feels more like a public slap in the face. Jail guaranteed my safety, and the specifics of my last arrest softened hearts that were once hard towards me. Nobody likes to see someone go down when they're making changes.

Freedom, on the other hand, births classic family conflict. Being at my brother's isn't easy. Buddy and Dorothy are used to things a certain way. Understandable. Everyone prefers peaceful living quarters. Mother-daughter rivalry, combined with the curiosity of a five-year-old, and the demands of an infant—collisions are constant. Who wouldn't want to throw four big babies out with their bothersome bathwater.

After three strenuous months, Azlynn and I find a cute little house. Living together is a touchy matter. Similar to the brisk removal of a corroded bandage. When ripped away without consideration, the scabs remain attached to the gauze part. After a month of bumps and bruises the flesh is scraped away. The once contented spots become open and sore. The whole deal can get obscene.

Thought our hurts were healed and that the past would be left there, but naked wounds are easily re-injured. Recovery's a delicate process. Requires the proper material—and no matter how good the treatment—time is a must.

★ ★ ★

In November my parents come for Jordan and my birthday. They take me to a friend's house. A beautiful spot on an inlet. Wasn't expecting such luxurious treatment. I lug Mom's suitcase toward the bedroom she'll be staying in. When I get to the top of the stairs, you'll never believe who's there. Dori!

My sister flew in from California for the occasion. Utterly astonished. No way to recreate for you the intense relief that shakes my soul as I hold her thin body near to my heart. We've spoken a bunch, but I certainly didn't expect this honored surprise.

We do sister stuff. Share our likes and hates. Tell secrets and jokes. I even cut her hair. She explains how chemotherapy has caused hair to grow on her face. With the plug to the waxer in my hand I say with a wink, "Have no fear, your sister is here." We chuckle together.

Mom walks in before I begin and explains how waxing her cheeks may cause her hair to grow in thicker. She makes eye contact with me and says, "Don't think I need to worry about that." Morbid reality bridles the fun. My warrior of a sister. So brave, yet unbelievably realistic. It's just not fair.

On the seventh, the family throws a wonderful party for me and my son. My sister owns a catering company. She's an incredible cook so the food is fab. It's an unbelievable night of family magic.

Before I know it our time is over. After a week of laughter and sorrow, taking hold and letting go, expectation and impossibility, Dori returns home. What a precious and priceless memory for me. The last time we're together.

I've learned to protect myself. Defense. It's important to keep the right kind of guard up. The adversary storms around on the sidelines like an angry referee. Always watching for the wrong move or some sorta interference. Thoughts haven't changed. And feelings? They just stumble around in the outfield hoping some showy pop-fly will gain them notice. Can't wait for the day they lose their footing and are too weak to show their ugly mugs.

My best strategy for the ever elusive answer is this: I must practice long and hard until I'm strong enough to outplay them. The better my skills get, the more feeble their attacks appear.

Justification, denial, logic. They sneak up on me and suggest I skip the bases and run straight for home-plate. But genuine victory won't be achieved if I abandon the process. Can't stop now.

I've spent my entire existence trying to live up to some outrageous standard. Not one that's been set by another, but one I put into effect for myself. We all have knowledge we choose to believe. Some accurate, some not.

As a child I felt misunderstood and dominated. The love I experienced came with restrictions. No such thing as unconditional acceptance. Basic needs that were left unmet sit on the bench spitting lies at me.

Time for me to make up my mind that I don't have to believe what I've always heard in my head. Just because I've got it memorized doesn't make it a fact.

Then come the feelings—pain, doubt, confusion, anger, fear. Normal responses. We're all washed-up in one way or the other. Consumed by various addictions. In circumstantial downpours we're known to throw up our hands in timeout and sprint towards the dugout of avoidance.

What will it take to beat this? How do I formulate a legitimate game plan?

★ ★ ★

The drinks I had at the wedding revived what AA refers to as "terminal uniqueness." We're all subject to this epidemic as well. A belief in the "onlys." I'm the only one who feels like this. The only one who has the answer. The only one who can get away with breaking the rules.

Living with my daughter is tough. Even as I write this next part, I can't believe it. After two months of hostile arguments and tedious faultfinding, I give in to desertion. I leave Azlynn's on Friday to get a drink with a friend. Unwind. No big deal. Handled it fine last time.

Half a bottle later I find myself caught in a delirious net that's free from inhibition. Divorced from caution, crack cocaine sings an alluring melody that draws me to it's bedside. Infatuated by my long-lost lover. Starstruck. Or should I say powerless.

After 24 hours of irrational circles, I have a moment of clarity. Though tempted to stay and frolic around in the ashes of fire and brimstone, I don't. Not because I can't, because I won't. Too sickening. Have to get back to the place I was. Break this repetitive pattern. How did I forget how much I hate this?

Saturday evening I do something different. U-turn. I stumble home and face the consequences. Not because there's no other choice, because I know this street ends in a brick wall.

Squashed by a betrayed expression from my daughter and the uneasy concern of my precious grandson, my outlook's demolished. Fooled again. This can't be happening. My camouflage fatigues are worn out. No longer a reliable decoy. Truth's vibrant colors can't be disguised. Gotta stop this cycle. Exhausted.

41

SAIL BABY SAIL

Baby's boat's the silver moon,
Sailing in the sky,
Sailing o'er the sea of sleep,
While the clouds float by.
Sail, baby, sail,
Out upon life's sea,
Only don't forget to sail
Back again to me.

I wake early Sunday morning to use the bathroom. Collapsing back into bed I stretch my legs toward the wooden slats above me on Pierce's bed. Better this bunkbed than the one in the county jail.

Jail! Probation! Oh my god, I have to call in.

I dial the number praying my officer's voice isn't the one on the recording. If it is, I'll have to drop a drug screen this morning. That's how drug offender probation's setup.

It's not her. Praise God. Impossible to comprehend the depth of His grace. You'd think He'd be exhausted by now. After a while you wonder if He's not just dumb. I mean what idiot does that? Just keeps believing for the best.

Maybe this is the acceptance I've always longed for? Approval that can only be given by someone who's perfect.

Revolted by the thought of me, I roll my face into my pillow and sob. For eighteen months I woke without this feeling.

My insides cringe with self-despise. This sinkhole of alienation is more than I can stomach. I never want to feel this again.

"You aren't meant to. It's unnecessary. My love for you is much more than you've understood it to be, Texas. Heaven's not some far-off dream of escape. I don't just give My perfection for your sin. I give My strength in your weakness. Joy in the midst of sorrow. Beauty's what I trade for ugliness. I give vibrant, vital, victorious life. Right here, right now. Today.

"It's a package deal. My offer is all. Everything you'll ever need. Kiss that inconsistent and demonic game goodbye. This is no dice roll. It's My promise to you, and I always keep My word. Always. Stop working like a slave; you're a citizen of the Kingdom. Remember? And I'm protective of what belongs to Me. You'll never be strong enough. Simply trust. Let Me be your King. I won't fail you.

"You've lost this match, but you don't have to be defeated in the battle. When will you learn to access My presence? The armies of heaven are waiting on My instruction. All I need is your permission. A white flag of surrender. I'll do the rest. What do you say?"

I've had the picture all wrong. The only guarantee in life is God. He's not this perplexing being that's above and beyond the universe. Someone or something that has absolute power over me. Although this is true of God, that's not where it ends. He's within, and all around. A force that continues to bring goodness, favor, and compassion. Magnificent.

An encourager, a friend, someone I can depend on. My protector, defender, and matchless resource. This world is fouled but He is flawless. When there's no way out, He's my deliverer. In Him I have power to accept and appreciate my circumstances. The shame of my past is no longer my burden. I give up.

This is where I draw the line. I'm making the choice to believe the truth no matter what my circumstances look or feel like. I'm sold out. No more resistance. I quit.

Not because I'm sick of jail or tired of the chase. Not because my parents are hurt or my children miss me. Not to silence the gossip or repair the damage. Not because drugs are illegal or immoral. Shouldn't and couldn't never have motivated me.

I want to do this for this reason and this reason alone...

I will never use drugs again because I refuse to be cut off from the One whose love has fixed every fracture and forgiven every failure.

I listened to every suggestion of the enemy for so long I believed him. There's no such thing as magical liberation. Besides, I'm already free and anything I hear that tells me different is a big fat nasty lie.

This last time I spent off drugs let me experience a special distance. New and unique separation from untruth. My mind began to see and believe who I truly am. Hope expanded. The instant I reverted to old behaviors all the old lies came back into view. This stark contrast allowed me to desire different enough to relinquish self-management.

"Stop looking at your shortcomings as lack, Sparkle. Without them you would never turn to Me. They're a gift. I love you enough to allow you to suffer. It's the only way you ever realize your need for Me. I left you with a void that only I can fill. When all other lights go out, I'm the One still shining."

★ ★ ★

...I've been totally coherent for three years now. Drug and alcohol free. Re-created. Transformed. Brand new. I have excitement and enthusiasm. Sometimes for no reason at all. I can find a remarkable contentment right in the center of ridiculous chaos. I have serenity, immunity, destiny. I know who I am and I like me.

I'm okay being alone but I'm also happy in a crowd. I wake up with wonder and amazement at who I've become and where I'm headed. Life is all that and I'm enthused to be involved in it. People believe in me and rely on me.

Sensational. The whole frickin' deal's good. I mean like totally radical.

All the feelings I ran from have no power anymore. They don't affect me. My old life was concentrated on a single goal. Drugs. This habit developed in me the ability to do whatever it takes to get where I'm headed. Life seems almost effortless now that I have the right focus.

God is passionate about me. What's important to me matters to Him. He allowed me to discover my purpose and then gave me the power to accomplish it.

I, my friend, have fallen head-over-heels in love with the Lover of my Soul. Jesus.

Instead of yelling His name when I'm freaked-out, pissed-off, or at my wits' end, I shout it in celebration. God is good. His love is sobering. Literally.

He's so taken with me He couldn't give up. My Creator, Champion, Confidant, Companion, and Constant Protection. He's enough to cover Tex-Ass—the whole state. And I've learned to bank on His much-needed assistance.

The greatest gift I've ever received is the secret strength found in proper reliance. Allegiance to the right cause. I no longer have a reason to hunt for relief. I just pack my waistband with weapons and take off for my War Room.

If this is all it takes to keep me from that fraudulent source of vulgar, vile, and vicious madness, I will never choose the other again.

I don't have to analyze. No calculating involved. Don't even have to know the direction or conclusion. All I have to do is linger in the open sky of possibilities. Remain attached to wisdom's string, follow the lead of my Savior's pull, and let the air of fresh potential take me to my intended destination. Can't help but enjoy the breeze, recognize the wonder, and welcome true abandon. It's not my responsibility to control things. I have learned to soar and glide through life and all its challenges. Fully relaxed. Completely at peace. Drifting on the winds of faith. High as a kite.

Free.

"For I am convinced that neither death, nor life, nor angels, nor principalities, nor things present, nor things to come, nor powers, nor height, nor depth, nor any other created thing, will be able to separate us from the love of God, which is in Christ Jesus our Lord" (Romans 8:38-39, *NASB*).

EPILOGUE

Today, as I write this revised epilogue, I'm dumbfounded. Until the 40th chapter of this book I was unable to opt-out when it came to drug use. What? There are only 41 chapters. Kinda makes you wonder where I am now, huh?

Thanks to grace, it's been an entire seven years since my last drink or drug. Incredible. My ministry and personal life have been coursing upward at a steady rate. Not too fast and not too slow. In varying, but infrequent increments, I wonder where I'm headed. But all the things I wrote in that last chapter have become true for me. I take it as it comes, roll with the punches, let life happen. For the most part, I could care less where I end up. Honestly. As long as my connection to Jesus is tight, I'm good.

★ ★ ★

We're all addicts. Anything we use to divert or dissolve our unwanted emotions has the power to allure our hearts repetitive-ly. Shopping, eating, lust, envy, anger. Again and again—until we're stuck. Many times I think we who've been openly seduced and sedated by the slavery of drug addiction have it better than you "functional" addicts.

My caverns of despair and regret have been deep and wide. Humongous already! This fact makes what most consider crises a drop in the bucket for me. Your boyfriend's been unfaithful? Lose him and find another. At least you're not in jail. That's what my brain screams.

I'm also good at saving and spending wisely. Something else I learned the wrong way, but God is using for good. He's amazing. All day, every day. Amazing. This skill has enabled me to manage my income and contributions so well that I have now ordered 7,500 new books. 5,000 of those books are going directly into 2,649 different institutions in the United States. Because each book counts for 30 people that means 150,000 inmates will have read my book within the next six months. Talk about more than you can ask or imagine. This is it.

Drug addicts ain't buying books. Not this week. And they're not reading them either. Not unless they're caged. Jails, prisons, rehabs, even high schools. That's where I go. I travel all over the country, telling my story and giving away books.

And lives are changing. Parents are learning what real love looks like and those who are bound have gained a hunger for freedom. High schoolers are reconsidering rebellion and Christians rethinking religion. Killer!

Jesus, Jesus, Jesus. Where would I be without Jesus? I'm sure I don't think of this as often as I should. Lord, You are my freedom. My hope and contentment. My this and that, my to and fro. All I want and all I'll ever need. I know this. I believe this. I love this. Thank you. All the voices that exist could never be enough to articulate what You mean to me.

Stay tuned. Working on the sequel now.

Feel what you feel till what you feel is healed